ROYAL YACHTS

ROYAL YACHTS

ALAN MAJOR

AMBERLEY

First published 2011

Amberley Publishing
Cirencester Road, Chalford,
Stroud, Gloucestershire, GL6 8PE

www.amberleybooks.com

Copyright © Alan Major 2011

The right of Alan Major to be identified as the Author
of this work has been asserted in accordance with the
Copyrights, Designs and Patents Act 1988.

British Library Cataloguing in Publication Data.
A catalogue record for this book is available from the British Library.

ISBN 978-1-4456-5784-4

Typeset in 10pt on 12pt Sabon.
Typesetting and Origination by Amberley Publishing.
Printed in the UK.

Contents

INTRODUCTION

My book has its roots in the 1970s. A lifetime interest in subjects nautical eventually resulted in my *Maritime Antiques Dictionary* being published in 1981. During those years, I had also gathered an archive of information and photographs concerning royal, imperial, state and presidential sailing and steam-powered yachts. The intended ambition was to combine these materials into a book and indeed I did prepare one. Unfortunately, two similar books appeared at that time and creamed off the market so no publisher was interested in mine. The material was all shelved to try again on a suitable occasion after time had passed.

Time did pass and it occurred to me that a 'suitable occasion' would be the sixtieth anniversary of the accession of Her Majesty Queen Elizabeth, our long-serving and hard-working monarch. I updated the manuscript text where required and added more photographs as illustrations. My thanks go to Campbell McCutcheon and the editorial staff of Amberley Publishing for converting it all into the book before you.

During my research, a number of ex-naval men who had served on the British royal yachts or had some connection with them got in touch with me, and their families wrote to me with details and memorabilia of their relatives' service. They also gave me photographs of vessels they served on and of the officers and crew with members of the Royal Family and Household: 'for your book on royal yachts'. It was the united opinion of them all that a worthy book about these ships should be written and that is, I said, what I hoped to achieve. Their names are listed in the Acknowledgments, but sadly many of those who helpfully assisted without thought of recompense have passed away without seeing the fruits of their support.

I am also most grateful to be able to record the fact that Her Majesty the Queen has granted me permission to include photographs of herself, Princess Margaret and other members of the Royal Family on board the *Victoria and Albert* (III). The late Prince Rainier III of Monaco kindly sent me photographs of the royal yachts of Monaco, and some of the European maritime museums have assisted with information and photographs.

In a sense, my book is also a memorial to those magnificent and often beautiful ships, symbols of a gracious era that has gone forever. I hope to have achieved my ambition of providing a worthy record of their life and times.

ALAN MAJOR

BY THE SAME AUTHOR

The Kentish Lights – the story of Kent's lightships and lighthouses
(S. B. Publications, 2000)

Maritime Antiques – An Illustrated Dictionary
(A. S. Barnes & Co., New York, 1981)

Princess Elizabeth on board HMS *Vanguard*. (J & C McCutcheon Collection)

ACKNOWLEDGEMENTS

The author gratefully acknowledges with his thanks the assistance of the following:

La Spezia Naval Museum, Italy, for information and the gift of Italian and Egyptian royal yacht photographs.

Capt. R. Steen Steensen, Marinehistorisk Selskab, Hellerup, Denmark, for information and the generous gift of his book, *The Ships of the Danish Kings*, 1972.

Cmdr. Richard Speer, Ships Historical Branch, Department of the Navy, Washington Navy Yard, USA, for information regarding US Presidential yachts.

Deutsche Museum, Munich, for information and the gift of a photograph of the *Hohenzollern*.

Colin S. White, MA, Royal Naval Museum, Portsmouth, regarding information and royal yacht figurehead photographs.

N. E. Upham, Assistant Keeper, Dept. of Ships, National Maritime Museum, Greenwich, for identifying ships on a photograph and for HMS *Surprise* information.

Capt. W. S. Mackay, Beaumont, Jersey, for information on British and foreign royal yachts.

Lewis V. Tyler, Southsea, former royal yacht crew member, for the gift of *Victoria and Albert* (III) Kiel Canal photograph; launching of the *Victoria and Albert* (III) at Pembroke photograph; and the Princesses Elizabeth and Margaret photograph.

Portsmouth News, Portsmouth, for permission to use their *Victoria and Albert* (III)/*Britannia* photograph.

Tomaso Gropallo, maritime author and historian, Genoa, for information and the gift of photographs.

Edna Colyer, Gosport, for information and the gift of photographs.

Ethel Pook, Alverstoke, Gosport, for information and the gift of photographs.

Beryl Powell, Havant, for loan and permission to use her *Victoria and Albert* (III) snapshots.

Mona Hatchett, Felixstowe, for information regarding *Osborne* (II) photograph.

S. Lilliman, Kempston, for use of *Osborne* (II) photograph.

Harold Parks, Sheerness, for gift of *Victoria and Albert* (III) photograph.

H. McLachlan, Dunoon, for gift of the 1935 *Mahroussa* postcard.

R. W. Cowl, York, for gift of *Mahroussa* and HMS *Surprise* photographs.

Andrew M. Berry, Colchester, for the gift of a photograph and identifying the ships on it.

William H. Lapthorn, Broadstairs, for information regarding royal yachts' histories.

Commander Brian Boxall-Hunt, OBE, RN, Royal Alfred Seafarers' Society, Banstead, for information regarding Belvedere House flag mast.

G. L. Orry, Chester, for the photograph of his model of the 1804 *Royal Sovereign*.

Peter Turrall, Marconi Veterans' Association, for information regarding Marconi's yacht, *Elettra*.

Campbell McCutcheon, for publishing the book and supplying images.

The author also gratefully acknowledges the generous assistance of the following with photographs, information and advice:

C. C. Penning, Head of Photograph Department, Nederlands Historisch Scheepvaart museum, Amsterdam.

J. van Beylen, Stad Antwerpen Nationaal Scheepvaartmuseum, Antwerp.

Henning Henningsen, Handels-og-Sofartmuseet Pa Kronborg, Helsingor, Denmark.

Nicolai Kirkebygring, Orlogsmuseet, Copenhagen.

Sjöhistoriska Museet (National Maritime Museum), Stockholm.

Pierre de Meslon, French Section of the World Ship Society, Asnières.

Jose Ma Martinez-Hidalgo, Museo Maritima, Barcelona.

A. de Carvalho Andrade, Museu de Marinha, Lisbon.

H. Murphy, Brixham, Devon.

The British Library, Canterbury City Library and archives staff.

Andrew Buckworth, Canterbury, for technical assistance regarding information.

Derek Chatfield, Swalecliffe, Kent, for technical assistance with information.

ROYAL YACHTS

ROYAL YACHTS OF EUROPE

Imperial Austria-Hungary: *Fantasie. Miramar. Greif. Rovenska/Elettra. U1.*
Belgium: *Alberta*, ex-*Margarita.*
Bulgaria: *Nadiejda.*
Denmark: *Slesvig. Dannebrog* (I). *Dannebrog* (II).
France: *L'Aigle. Jerome Napoleon. La Reine Hortense.*
Germany: *Kaiseradler. Grille. Hohenzollern,* 1892. *Hohenzollern,* 1914.
    Meteor I-V.
Great Britain: *The White Ship (Le Blanche Nef). Trench le Mer. Queen. George.*
    Christopher. Thomas. Grace de Dieu. John. Trinity Royal. King's Chamber.
    Katherine Pleasaunce. Disdain. Prince Royal. Mary. Katherine. Merlin. Anne.
    Henrietta. Surprise/Royal Escape. Saudadoes. Kitchen. Cleveland. Portsmouth.
    Fubbs. Charlot. Jamie/Jemmy. Charles. Charles (II). *Mary* (II). *Katherine*
    (II). *Henrietta* (II). *Isabella. Isabella* (II). *Isabella Bezan. Anne. Bezan. Navy.*
    Merlin. Monmouth. Quinborow. Deale. William and Mary. Transport Royal:
    Peregrine Galley/Carolina/Royal Caroline. Squirrel. Scout. Queenborough.
    Isle of Wight. Fubbs (II). *Isabella* (II). *Charlot* (II). *Augusta. Old Portsmouth/*
    Medina. Portsmouth (II). *Drake. Bolton. Dublin. Princess Mary/Betsy Cairns.*
    Chatham. Katherine (III). *Fubbs* (III). *Mary* (III). *Queenborough* (II) and (III).
    Peregrine Sloop. Royal Charlotte. Drake (II). *Chatham* (II). *Portsmouth* (III).
    Dorset. Plymouth. Royal Sovereign. Princess Augusta. William and Mary (II).
    Chatham (III). *Plymouth* (II). *William and Mary* (III). *Royal George. Prince*
    Regent. Royal Charlotte (II). *Royal Adelaide.*
Edward VII's sailing craft: *Dagmar. Princess. Alexandra. Zenobia. Hildegarde.*
    Formosa. Aline. Bloodhound. The White Lady. Britannia cutter. Bluebottle.
    Victoria and Albert (I)/*Osborne. Victoria and Albert* (II). *Fairy. Elfin. Alberta.*
    Alexandra. Osborne (II). *Victoria and Albert* (III). *Britannia.*
Temporary royal yachts: HMS *Ariadne. Ophir. Medina.* HMS *Renown. Empress*
    of Australia. Empress of Britain. HMS *Vanguard. Gothic.* HMS *Surprise.*
Greece: *Spaktena.*
Italy: *Jela. Savoia* (I). *Savoia* (II). *Trinacria.*
Monaco: *Albercaro* (II). *Princess Alice* (I). *Princess Alice* (II). *Carostephal. Costa*
    del Sol. Hirondelle (I). *Hirondelle* (II). *Deo Juvante* (II). *Stalco. Cecelia.*
Netherlands: *De Leeuw. Piet Hein. Valk.*

Norway: *Norge.*
Portugal: *Amelia* (I). *Amelia* (II). *Amelia* (III). *Madedja. Yacoma. Aura. Lia*, ex-*Mida. Nautilus. Sado*, ex-*Banshee. Sirius. Veloz.*
Roumania: *Luceafarul*, ex-*Nahlin*, ex-*Libertatea.*
Imperial Russia: *Livadia. Pole Star. Standart.*
Spain: *Giralda. Tontine. Hispania. Barandil.*
Sweden: *Amphion. Drott.*
Yugoslavia: *Dubrovnik. Dragor. Vila.*

ROYAL YACHTS OUTSIDE EUROPE

Egypt: *Cleopatra. Khassed Kheir. Mahroussa. Safa-el-Bahr.*
Turkey: *Teshrifiyeh. Erthogroul. Savarona.*
Zanzibar: *Nyanza.*

PRESIDENTIAL, STATE AND MISCELLANEOUS YACHTS

Argentine Republic: *Presidente Sarmiento.*
United States of America: *Mayflower. Despatch. Dolphin. Sylph. Sequoia. Potomac. Williamsburg.*
Smaller craft: *Dollar* then named *Margie, Margaret T, Susan Elaine, Patrick J. Julie.* the *Barbara Anne* later *Honey Fitz.*

The *Medina*, a temporary royal yacht, with HMS *Victory* in the background.
(J & C McCutcheon Collection)

FROM SAIL TO STEAM

A dictionary definition of a modern yacht is 'a craft, whether propelled by sails or by mechanical power, designed for pleasure cruising'. The word comes from the Old Dutch *jacht* with two original meanings. One was hunt – *ter jacht gaen* – to go a-hunting. Secondly, *jacht* was a light, swift sailing ship. A *jachtschip* was 'a ship for chasing'. A *statenjacht*, however, was 'a light sailing ship for pleasure'. All were eventually corrupted by English speech into yacht.

In earliest maritime history, there were special ships designed, built set aside for the conveyance of kings, queens, emperors, ambassadors and various categories of governing personage to and from their domain as a visible sign of their apparent importance, power and wealth. These vessels were not just for this purpose. They had a use for political show, embarking and disembarking visiting royalty and high-ranking nobility. In wartime, they were adapted and put into service to cross the English Channel or North Sea to Europe. They had the occasional use for trading purposes, where the presence of the king's personal vessel indicated how important the mission was to him politically.

The early kings, Anglo-Saxon and Norman, were no exception to this situation and had single-masted, sail-powered or oar-powered vessels, or both means of locomotion for extra speed or when the wind was light. It is a popular image, the sighting of these 'longships', with raised ramming bows adorned with fearsome beasts or birds, lined with shields, with a square striped sail or, in the case of the king's ship, a purple sail to note his whereabouts in the fleet, being rowed and manned by equally fearsome-looking men, striking dread into those on the shore.

The king known for one of the most famous battles and dates in English history, William the Conqueror (1027–87, the Battle of Hastings, 1066), sailed to invade England on his personal ship *Mora*, depicted on the Bayeux Tapestry. His youngest son, Henry I (1100–35), had his own ship, *La Blanche Nef* (*The White Ship*), so-called due to its paintwork and sail. Sadly it was the cause of the death of his only legitimate son, seventeen-year-old William. Prince William and his brother Richard, his noble friends and servants embarked on the ship at Barfleur, Normandy, on 25 November 1120 and set off for England. Henry had sailed earlier in a different ship. One version of the incident states that most of the crew and passengers had imbibed wine too well. Control of the ship was lost, a rock was struck, and the ship was holed and quickly sank. All but one person on it perished. A second version suggests the ship was caught in a sudden violent gale that sprang up and drove it onto the Goodwin Sands off the East Kent coast opposite Deal, where it was held by the sand and foundered. Again almost all aboard were drowned, including Prince William. It is reputed that in certain inclement sea conditions a ghost *White Ship* still drives onto the Sands. Quite normal, level-headed seafarers have seen it doing so.

The importance of the Master (Captain) in charge of the monarch's personal ship is indicated by Henry II (1154–89), who, for his services, gave Hugh Le Bec from Normandy, Master of Henry's ship, a manor with considerable land acreage near Bekesbourne, Canterbury.

In the twelfth century, Richard I (1189–99) had *Trench Le Mer*, 'Cleave the Sea', as his personal ship. He sailed on it with various warships on the Third Crusade from England to the Mediterranean to take part in a sea battle against the Saracens off Acre, resulting in the Crusaders capturing that port.

Henry III (1216–72) had two royal ships, known as the King's Great Ships, or the King's Galleys. They were the *Queen* and the *Cardinal*, although the latter had not started as a King's Ship but, as may be indicated by its name, had been seized from the Portuguese.

In his un-named 'Royal Shippe', Edward I (1272–1307) intended a romantic use. Margaret, 'The Maid of Norway', daughter of the King of Norway, but also heiress to all Scotland, was due to marry Edward's son, also Edward. So in 1290, Edward's 'Royal Shippe' was victualled and stocked with necessities to sail from Yarmouth to Norway, to embark Margaret and transport her to England for her marriage. While doing so, in violent weather, the ship sank and Margaret, with many of her retinue and crew, was drowned.

The French were frequently rebellious during Edward III's reign (1327–77) so he had, in consequence, to sail to France to subdue them. One of his 'Great Shippes' that he used was *George*, perhaps named after England's patron saint. Two others, *Christopher* and *Thomas*, were a type of vessel known as a cog. All were based at Sandwich, Kent, then a large, flourishing port that had had more than its share of raids from France. In 1347, returning from such a venture, many of the 'Great Shippes' were caught in a severe storm. The King, on *George*, arrived safely off the bay into Sandwich, but many vessels were lost with their complement of knights, servants and crew. Later, as if to show the flag to the French and that we still had a fleet, in 1372, Edward sailed from Sandwich in the *Grace de Dieu*, with an escort, to voyage up and down the coast of Normandy and Brittany.

Henry IV (1399–1413) let everyone witnessing know who was on board his ship, also a cog, *John*. The sail had his coat of arms embroidered on it. The capstan in the bows, for hauling up an anchor, was carved with three fleur-de-lis (representations of the garden lily or iris, the armorial bearing of the Kings of France from 1147). The summit of the mast bore a gilded replica of the crown and sceptre, and the king's crest, a crowned lion. The royal banner, some streamers and eight *guidons* (pennants or small flags) flew on the mast.

Henry V (1413–22), of Agincourt fame, assembled some 1,400 ships at Southampton for his expedition into France and sailed on his *Trinity Royal* on 10 August 1415 for the battle. Having achieved his intention against the French army, he sailed from Calais for Dover on 16 November, but the sea was very rough and two of his ships with some of his victorious army sank, and all on board were lost. The King had a number of other ships, one of them also being a *Grace a Dieu*, believed to be the first ship with two masts to be used by royalty in English waters. It had been customary for several of the English kings to have royal purple sails on their own ship. Henry V was the last to do so. When he sailed on his ship *King's Chamber* from France to England, the silken sail was royal purple embroidered with the Arms of England and France, in gold thread.

It seems he spared no expense. However, young Henry VI (1422–61) put most of His Majesty's personally owned ships up for sale. Why? Was he no sailor? The reason was more mundane. It was to pay off his father's expenditure on his 'war ships', among other debts.

Henry VIII (1509–47) was another king who used his ships to put on a show to indicate England was the equal of other European seafaring nations. How impressive the scene must have looked when the royal fleet set sail from Dover for Calais on 31 May 1520, eventually to meet Francis I, King of France, on 7 June at Andren, near Calais – later called the Field of the Cloth of Gold by historians. The two monarchs were attended by the flower of the nobility and knighthood of both nations. Each had their retinue and their glittering and gilded banners bearing their arms of chivalry. The King's own ship, the 100-ton *Katherine Pleasaunce*, built at Deptford 1514, took part; the sails and streaming pennants made of gold cloth, the ship was also adorned with royal standards and much of the upperworks artistically gilded.

The indomitable Queen Elizabeth I (1558–1603) did not, it seems, particularly like being on board ship and had no need to travel by ship beyond the bounds of England. She did sail on the Thames when required by duty to do so and is believed to have had a 'shippe', the *Rat O'Wight*, a curious name, built at Shamford, Isle of Wight, for this purpose.

The first monarch of England and Scotland to have had a small royal yacht built, as a gift for a child, is reputed to be James VI and I (1603–25), for his ten-year-old son, Henry, Prince of Wales. The shipwright, Commissioner Phineas Pett, related how this occurred in his memoirs:

> About January 15th, 1604, a letter was sent post haste to Chatham from my Honourable Lord Admiral Howard, Lord High Admiral, commanding me with all possible speed to build a little vessel for the young Prince Henry to disport himself in about London Bridge and acquaint His Grace with shipping and the manner of that element; setting me down the proportions and the manner of garnishings, which was to be like the work of the *Ark Royal*, battlementwise. This little ship was in length 25 feet by the keel and in breadth 12 feet, garnished with painting and carving, both within board and without, very curiously, according to his Lordship's directions.

This small 'royal yacht' was launched at Chatham on 6 March with much ceremony and sailed up the Thames to the Tower of London, where Prince Henry and the Lord High Admiral both 'viewed it agreeably'. Next day the Prince visited it again with the Lord High Admiral to throw 'a greate bowle of wine' against its bows and name it *Disdain*. The *Disdain* was happily used by the Prince and other royal children. In June 1612, King James sent an order to Pett for another much larger ship. It was to be a seagoing craft, 72 feet long, 24 feet beam and 11 feet draught, ship-rigged with three masts. When not in royal use, it was to act as a tender for the fifty-five-gun man-of-war *Prince Royal*, also built by King James. Sadly, young Prince Henry died before the later 'royal yacht' was launched.

Curiously, despite all the previously mentioned vessels being built for the king, the word *yacht* was apparently unknown in England until the seventeenth century. Then it was used because of a royal event. After Charles II (then Charles, Prince of Wales) had fled from England to Fécamp, France, then to Holland in 1651, life was not too arduous for him, it seems. Being nautically minded and skilled, he filled in some of his time in exile by sailing with his brother, James, in *statenjachts*. He was so satisfied with their handling qualities that, on his restoration to the

English throne in 1660, the Burgomaster of Amsterdam, on behalf of the city of Amsterdam and the Dutch people, presented him with an example, which had been built in 1658. It was obtained from the Dutch Admiralty Board and made ready for its royal owner, complete with the carving, gilding and decoration that Charles enjoyed. He brought it to England on 12 August 1660. This can rightly claim to be the first true royal yacht. From this example to the last – *Britannia* – there were to be eighty-three royal yachts.

The 100-ton, cutter-or-yacht-rigged Dutch State craft was 52 feet at the keel, had a beam of 19 feet, a depth in hold of 7 feet 7 inches, and was fitted with leeboards (wooden frames fastened over the lee side of flat-bottomed craft to prevent them losing leeway and deviation from a true course, thus losing time), which gave the craft a light draught of 3 feet. Leeboards at that time were a curiosity in England and later dispensed with in favour of a fixed keel. It also carried eight three-pounder guns, four on each side, mainly for signalling use, but to be used in defence should the vessel be attacked while sailing in the English Channel and Thames Estuary. The stern cabin was richly adorned with gilded figures and scrollwork. On the bows the figurehead was a leaping unicorn; on the stern were the royal arms. Charles named the craft *Mary*, after his sister, the Princess Royal. In 1661, *Mary* was transferred to the Royal Navy. It came to a tragic end, being wrecked in fog on the Skerries rocks, seven miles off Holyhead, Anglesey, on 4 April 1675.

Samuel Pepys, naval administrator on the Naval Board, wrote in his diary regarding a visit to *Mary*, on 8 November 1660: 'On board the royal yacht which is indeed the finest thing I saw for neatness and room in so small a vessel. Mr Pett, Commissioner, is to make one to outdo this for the honour of the country, which I fear he will scarce better.'

Three hundred years later in 1975, the wreck of *Mary* was found by diver members of the Chorley and Merseyside branch of the British Sub Aqua Club. Its discovery revealed the events of the still-unknown tragedy. After *Mary* had been transferred to the Royal Navy, it was used to convey passengers to various destinations, notably to and from Holyhead and Dublin. On the day of the loss of *Mary*, it was taking the Earl of Meath, Lord Ardee, and the Earl of Ardglass and their retinue from Dublin to Chester. As it sank some of the survivors were able to get onto the rocks, but thirty-five, including the Earl of Meath, were drowned. Divers had already recovered several three-pounder guns and other artefacts when in the cabin they discovered a skeleton. The bones had been well preserved by iron released from the ballast. They were removed and identified at Liverpool University's Department of Anatomy as those of a twenty-year-old woman. It is assumed that when *Mary* foundered and heeled over, the unfortunate woman had been trapped.

The *Mary* was the first of twenty-six royal yachts in the reign of Charles II, but not all were entirely for royal use only. The next example, this time built on his orders, was *Katherine*, designed and constructed at Deptford in 1661 by Surveyor Commissioner, Peter Pett, one of several generations of the famous family of ship designers and builders, at a cost of £1,335. This 94-ton, one-masted yacht, 49 feet at the keel, beam of 19 feet, with an in-hold depth of 7 feet, making leeboards unnecessary, armed with eight three-pounder guns, was named *Katherine* by Charles after his wife, Katherine of Braganza, Infanta of Portugal, whom he married at Portsmouth in 1662. In 1670, Charles challenged the Dutch Envoy to England, who had claimed his yacht was the fastest in Europe, to a race against the *Katherine* for a £500 wager. The Dutch Envoy declined to accept because he said it would be 'unseemly to race against the King of England and possibly beat him'. A sentiment not shared by others, some crowned heads in Europe particularly, in more recent times.

The alleged failure of some Dutch ships to acknowledge and salute *Merlin*, one of Charles II's royal yachts that also undertook other duties, led to the Third Anglo-Dutch War in 1672. In August 1673, at the Battle of Texel, *Katherine* was ignominiously captured by Dutch ships. In November 1674, the Dutch returned the yacht, rather bizarrely as a gift from the Prince of Orange, to try to improve relations between the two countries. Charles II did not particularly want it back. He had already ordered a replacement *Katherine* (II) at Chatham, so the original ended up being used by the Navy's Ordnance Board.

Not to be outdone by the King, his brother, James, Duke of York, Lord High Admiral of England, later James II, had the 100-ton *Anne* built for his personal use at Woolwich in 1661. It was designed and constructed by Surveyor Christopher Pett, Peter Pett's brother. Similar to *Katherine*, it was 52 feet at the keel, had a beam of 19 feet, a depth in hold of 7 feet, and was named after James's wife, Anne, Duchess of York. It was sold off in 1686.

Another royal yacht that had a mixed career was the 104-ton *Henrietta*. Designed and built in 1663 at Woolwich by Surveyor Christopher Pett, it was 52 feet at the keel, had a beam of 19 feet 6 inches, a depth in hold of 7 feet, armed with eight three-pounder guns, and was named after Henrietta Maria (1609–69), the King's mother, or possibly Henriette Anne, his sister, the Duchess of Orléans. This royal yacht was also involved in the Battle of Texel, but was sunk by the Dutch fleet. Presumably this was achieved entirely by gunfire, but were there other factors? During its construction, considerable extra ballast of lead and shot was required to maintain the ship on a straight and steady course in its trials.

One of the problems with wooden-hulled ships was that they were prey to the Teredo shipworms that attached themselves to, and bored into, the hull timbers. When present in large numbers, the ship's hull is weakened by their tunnels. Some ships had the reputation of only being held together by the shipworms. Numerous methods were used to try to prevent shipworm penetration, and in March 1671, Charles II visited Sheerness Dockyard to see lead sheets being attached to the hull of *Henrietta* 'to stoppe ye wormes'. It is believed to have been one of the first ships on which this method was tried as an alternative to powdered glass mixed with pitch paint. For a period this would be a success, but eventually corrosion occurred on the iron nails securing the lead sheets and while under way the sheets tended to drop off. The same occurred when copper sheathing was used. The lead was also extra weight that could affect the manoeuvrability of the ship.

After the Battle of Worcester, Charles II had escaped on 15 October 1651, from Brighton (Brighthelmstone) to Fécamp, France, then to Holland aboard *Surprise*, a small coasting vessel. Some sources say this ship was a brig or collier, but I am inclined to a hoy or a smack, these being used in southern coastal waters. On his restoration to the English throne in 1660, despite having a reputation as a licentious wastrel, he was also loyal and sentimental, and became angry when his seamen were not paid. He had bought *Surprise* from Captain Tattersall, who owned it, and had taken Charles to France; he then had it converted to a royal yacht and appropriately renamed the 34-ton ship *Royal Escape*. Its dimensions were 30 feet 6 inches at the keel, a beam of 14 feet 3 inches, and a depth in the hold of 7 feet. The King used it for various royal occasions and had such affection for this ship, realising how important it had been to his destiny, he had it moored on the Thames near to Whitehall Palace where he could see it daily from his rooms. In 1673, the *Royal Escape* was handed over to the Royal Navy and served therein for another forty years.

The first royal yacht of several built at Portsmouth was the 86-ton *Saudadoes*, designed and built in 1670 by Surveyor Sir Anthony Deane. It had a length at the keel of 50 feet, had a beam of 18 feet, a depth in the hold of 8 feet, and was armed with eight three-pounder guns. On 14 April 1670, the Queen Katherine named 'her' ship at Deptford. As she was Portuguese, the daughter of King John IV, she chose a Portuguese name, which basically means 'good wishes' or 'good luck', or rather curiously, in another sense, 'intense longing'. It was nicknamed by the public 'Queen Katherine's Little Ship'. It was intended mainly for the use of the Queen and her lady friends, as the *Royal Escape* was for her husband, Charles, and his friends. Katherine developed a fond affection for her own royal yacht and used it for upriver jaunts. She never ventured too far downriver. However, she had the use of *Saudadoes* for only about three years, after which it was transferred into service with the Royal Navy. In 1673, it was rebuilt as a 180-ton man-of-war, possibly to help make up for losses in the Third Anglo-Dutch war. *Saudadoes* took part in the Battle of Bantry Bay when Ireland was invaded by James II and was captured off Cape Barfleur, Normandy, by a French man-of-war in 1696.

A seeming oddity – in name and use – for a royal yacht, although appropriate, was the 103-ton *Kitchen*. As its name implies, this ship accompanied the royal yachts and accommodated the royal cooks and various other kitchen staff and servants who were required to prepare the food and serve it on the royal yachts. Built in 1674 at Rotherhithe by Surveyor William Castle, it had a length at the keel of 52 feet, had a beam of 19 feet 4 inches, a depth in the hold of 8 feet 6 inches, was single-masted and was armed in peacetime with six three-pounder guns. Obvious when thought about, these early royal yachts, small in size and accommodation, would not have had the catering facilities to wine and dine royalty, noblemen, foreign monarchs and ambassadors to a standard they expected. So the Dutch came up with a floating solution in the kitchen boat. On these were the bakers, cooks, other kitchen staff, stewards, and also the ovens and stoves necessary to prepare, cook and serve the food. Charles experienced these during his exile in Holland and on returning to England he had a ketch, *Roe*, requisitioned and converted to a sort of kitchen boat, renaming it *Roe Kitchen*. It proved a success, so in 1670 Charles ordered *Kitchen*. In 1692, *Kitchen* was converted to a 'bomb vessel' or 'bombardment vessel', the latter being the better name. In these the hulls were strengthened and armed with mortars for sailing close inshore and bombarding its target. Six years later, *Kitchen* was sold out of the Royal Navy.

Charles, being the 'Merry Monarch' and having a fondness for a variety of ladies of all social levels, not surprisingly followed a custom that still prevails in modern times of honouring a wife or girlfriend in some tangible way – in Charles's case naming some of the royal yachts after his mistresses.

The first example was the 107-ton *Cleveland*, built at Portsmouth in 1671 by Surveyor Sir Anthony Deane, which had a length at the keel of 53 feet 4 inches, a beam of 20 feet 6 inches, a depth in the hold of 7 feet 9 inches, and was armed with eight three-pounder guns. In August 1670, Charles II had made his married mistress Barbara Villiers the Duchess of Cleveland, Countess of Southampton and Baroness Nonsuch and named this royal yacht after her. In 1685, *Cleveland* was transferred to service with the Ordnance Office.

The next royal yacht with mistress associations was the 133-ton *Portsmouth*, designed and built in 1674 at Woolwich by Surveyor Phineas Pett. It had a length at the keel of 57 feet, had a beam of 20 feet, a depth in the hold of 7 feet 4 inches, and was single-masted and armed with eight three-pounder guns. In February 1673, Charles created his mistress, Louise de Keroualle, the Duchess of Portsmouth, Countess of Fareham and Lady Petersfield, and in 1674 named this royal yacht after her. In 1688, *Portsmouth* was transferred to naval service and converted to a 'bomb vessel'. During the Great Gale of November 1703, it was one of the hundreds of ships sunk or wrecked, its demise being at The Nore sandbank in the Thames Estuary.

Yet another 'mistress' royal yacht, although the same mistress, was the 148-ton *Fubbs*, designed by Surveyor Sir Phineas Pett and built at Greenwich in 1682. It had a length on the gundeck of 73 feet 6 inches, a length at the keel of 63 feet, a beam of 21 feet, a depth in the hold of 9 feet 6 inches, was two-masted, ketch rigged and armed with twelve three-pounder guns. It was the second royal yacht named after mistress Louise de Keroualle, Duchess of Portsmouth. This may have been so-called at the cheeky whim of Charles, the expressive Old English 'fubby' meaning 'plump', 'chubby'. Louise had plump cheeks, in other words 'fubby', the King's pet name for her being Fubbs. Charles also created his son by Louise the Duke of Richmond and Hereditary High Admiral of Scotland.

Due to the ship's speed and sailing qualities, *Fubbs* was the royal yacht Charles most enjoyed being on for ventures. On 30 June 1683, Charles and his brother James sailed *Fubbs* from Whitehall down the Thames, their destination Dover. The party aboard included the Reverend John Gostling of the Chapel Royal. It seems a good time was being had by all. Charles and Gostling were rumbustiously singing to the accompaniment of James playing a guitar. However, after sailing past Margate and round North Foreland, *Fubbs* was involved in a sudden squall and heeled over. Only a concerted effort by all on board prevented *Fubbs* from foundering before deliberate beaching in a bay on the Kent coast, known at the time as the Bay of St Bartholomew, with an entrance from the shore. Nearby at Bradstowe (Broadstairs) is the medieval Chapel of St Mary, Our Lady of Bradstowe, where a light in a blue glass lantern was displayed to be seen at sea and all seafarers who sailed past lowered their sails in salutation. In celebration of the King's safe deliverance, the entrance was renamed Kingsgate, as it is today. In 1724, *Fubbs* was rebuilt to continue in service until 1770, for a time being used as an accommodation ship for officers, then as a dispatch ship in the Royal Navy.

Not named after a mistress but a daughter – Charlotte, Countess of Yarmouth – who Charles had fathered with his mistress, Barbara Villiers, was the 142-ton *Charlot*, built in 1677 at Woolwich and designed by Surveyor Thomas Shish. It had a length at the keel of 61 feet 9 inches, a beam of 21 feet, a depth in the hold of 9 feet, was single-masted and armed with eight three-pounder guns. It was employed on short voyages, one being the sailing of Princess, later Queen, Mary, under escort to Holland, after her marriage to William, Prince of Orange, in 1677. The *Charlot* was eventually transferred into the service of the Lord Lieutenant of Ireland, 1701 to 1709, as his official yacht at Dublin. In 1710, it was taken into Deptford Dockyard to be rebuilt.

Not named after a mistress either but a son, James, Duke of Monmouth, whom Charles had fathered with mistress Lucy Walter, was the 27-ton *Jamie/Jemmy*, designed and built in 1662 at Lambeth by Surveyor Commissioner Pett. It had a length at the keel of 31 feet, a beam of 12 feet 6 inches, a depth in the hold of 6 feet and was armed with four guns. *Jamie* had a very long sailing life of some sixty years, before being broken up in 1721.

As so many of the royal yachts were named after various people and places, it was only right that two were named after Charles himself. The first was the 38-ton *Charles*, built Woolwich, 1662, by Surveyor Christopher Pett. It had a length at the keel of 36 feet, a beam of 14 feet, a depth in the hold of 7 feet, was single-masted and armed with six three-pounder guns. The King used it only for a short time before it was exchanged with the Ordnance Office for their smack *Tower*. The second, the 120-ton *Charles* (II), was designed and built in 1675 at Rotherhithe by Surveyor Sir Anthony Deane. It had a length at the keel of 54 feet, a beam of 20 feet 6 inches, a depth in the hold of 7 feet 9 inches, was single-masted and armed with eight three-pounder guns. It was one of several royal yachts that accompanied *Charlot* with Princess Mary and *Mary* (II) with her husband Prince William of Orange aboard back to Holland after their marriage in England in 1677. In November 1678, *Charles* (II) was wrecked on the Dutch coast.

King Charles II is rightly regarded as the 'Father' of yachting in England, as much for his enthusiasm for the sport and encouragement of it, as for twenty-six royal yachts that he had built during his lifetime and in whose construction and use he was keenly involved.

Other royal yachts of this period included: the 135-ton *Katherine* (II), designed and built at Chatham in 1674 by Surveyor Sir Phineas Pett. It had a length at the keel of 56 feet, a beam of 21 feet 4 inches, a depth in the hold of 8 feet 6 inches, was single-masted and armed with eight three-pounder guns. It was named after the first *Katherine*, which had been captured at the Battle of Texel by the Dutch in 1673. It was rebuilt in the reign of George I, 1720. The 166-ton *Mary* (II) was designed and built at Chatham in 1677 by Surveyor Sir Phineas Pett. It had a length at the keel of 66 feet 6 inches, a beam of 21 feet 6 inches, a depth in the hold of 8 feet 9 inches, was single-masted and armed with eight three-pounder guns. It was named after the first *Mary* wrecked off Holyhead, Anglesey, in 1675. In November 1677, *Mary* (II) conveyed William and Mary from Erith to Holland after their marriage. Sheerness Castle fired a gun salute as they passed with the fleet, which included *Charlot*, and anchored off Margate for the night, then all proceeded to Holland. The *Mary* (II) conveyed Mary, now Queen, from Holland to Greenwich to join William III in February 1689. The 162-ton *Henrietta* (II), designed and built at Woolwich in 1679 by Surveyor Thomas Shish, had a length at the keel of 65 feet, a beam of 21 feet 8 inches, a depth in the hold of 8 feet 3 inches, was single-masted and armed with eight three-pounder guns. It was named after the first *Henrietta* sunk by the Dutch during the Third Anglo-Dutch War, 1673. The 114-ton *Isabella*, designed and built at Greenwich 1683 by Surveyor Sir Phineas Pett, had a length at the keel of 60 feet, a beam of 18 feet 11 inches, a depth in the hold of 8 feet 11 inches, was single-masted, ketch-rigged and armed with eight three-pounder guns. It was broken up in 1702 and *Isabella* (II) was built at Deptford in 1703, during the reign of Queen Anne. The 52-ton *Isabella Bezan* was for a short time also *Isabella*; designed and built in Chatham, in 1680, by Surveyor Sir Phineas Pett. It had a length at the keel of 46 feet, a beam of 16 feet, a depth in the hold unknown and its armament is unknown. It was later renamed *Anne* and sold in 1683 to Surveyor Sir Phineas Pett, apparently in lieu of part of the cost of building the 1683 *Isabella*, this arrangement was unsurprisingly not pleasing to Surveyor Pett, stuck with an ex-royal yacht. The 100-ton *Anne* was built at Woolwich in 1661 by Surveyor Christopher Pett, as the 'personal use only' royal yacht of James, Duke of York, in his capacity as Lord High Admiral. It had a length at the keel of 52 feet, a beam of 19 feet, a depth in the hold of 7 feet, was single-masted and armed with eight three-pounder guns. It was named after his wife Anne. When James was crowned James II, this royal yacht was sold in 1686 into long service with the London Customs House. The 35-ton *Bezan*, built in Holland in 1661, had a length at the keel of 34 feet, a beam of 14 feet, a depth in the hold of 7 feet and was single-masted, its armament is unknown. It was given as a gift by the Dutch Government to Charles II in the hope of cementing friendship and trade between the two countries. The Dutch word *bezaan* means mizzen-sail. The *Bezan* was sold out of royal service in 1686 and broken up at Deptford in 1687. The 74-ton *Navy*, built in Rotherhithe, in 1666, by Surveyor William Castle, may have been so-named by Charles II to show his support for his Royal Navy. It had a length at the keel of 48 feet, a beam of 17 feet, a depth in the hold of 7 feet 7 inches and was armed with eight three-pounder guns. The *Navy* was one of the royal yachts among the fleet escorting Princess Mary and William, Prince of Orange, back to Holland after their marriage in 1677. Later it was transferred to the service of the Lord Lieutenant of Ireland at Dublin, 1689 to 1693, being sold in 1698.

The 109-ton *Merlin* (possibly named after the bird of prey), built in Rotherhithe, in 1666, by Surveyor Jonas Shish, was the royal yacht that, while en route to England in 1671, was discourteously ignored by the passing Dutch fleet, who refused to salute the English flag and thus bow to English sovereignty in the Channel, an insult that was just one cause of the Third Anglo-Dutch war. It had a length at the keel of 53 feet, a beam of 19 feet 6 inches, a depth in the hold of 8 feet, was sail rigged as a galliot (a fast type of ship moved by sails and oars) and armed with eight three-pounder guns. Later *Merlin* was loaned by Charles II as one of two royal yachts employed, at his suggestion, to make new charts of the British coastline and coastal waters in 1681 and 1682.

Also built at Rotherhithe in 1666, this time by Surveyor William Castle, was the 103-ton *Monmouth*. It had a length at the keel of 52 feet, a beam of 19 feet 6 inches, a depth in the hold of 8 feet and was armed with eight three-pounder guns. It was named after James, Duke of Monmouth, the son Charles fathered with his mistress Lucy Walter. This was the second royal yacht employed to the making of new charts of the British coastline and coastal waters, 1683 to 1688. Later it was used as a despatch boat between England and Ireland, being sold off in 1698.

The 29-ton *Quinborow* was built at Chatham in 1671 by Surveyor Phineas Pett within sight of the port it was named after – Queenborough, Isle of Sheppey – that by its own name indicates it had earlier royal associations. It had a length at the keel of 30 feet, a beam of 13 feet 4 inches, and a depth in the hold of 6 feet 6 inches and was armed with four three-pounder guns. It was used mainly as a tender for larger royal yachts and not for the king's personal use, being sold in 1719.

Two years later, two more small royal yachts were built on the orders of Charles II, but only for various royal services, not by himself or his family. The 28-ton *Deale*, built in Woolwich in 1673 by Surveyor Phineas Pett, had a length at the keel of 32 feet, a beam of 13 feet, a depth in the hold of 6 feet and was armed with four three-pounder guns. It is assumed it was named after Deal port and dockyard on the east coast of Kent, but probably used as a service yacht in Chatham or Sheerness Dockyards. The 30-ton *Isle of Wight*, built in Portsmouth in 1673 by Surveyor Mr Furzer, had a length at the keel of 33 feet, a beam of 12 feet 6 inches, a depth in the hold of 6 feet and was armed with four three-pounder guns. Named after where it was to be used, in the service of the Governor of the Isle of Wight.

James II (1685–88), despite being nautically enthusiastic and using the royal yachts in Charles's reign as his own, soon reduced their number; in 1686 he sold *Anne* and *Bezan*. In the year he died, 1688, he sold *Deale*, with *Portsmouth* being rebuilt as a 'bomb-vessel'.

The trend of using royal yachts continued into the reign of William III and Mary, who not only maintained fourteen of the ships they inherited, but built new examples. William III (reigned 1689–1702) was Stadtholder of Holland as well as King of England. This necessitated considerable movement of the royal yachts on royal business in Holland as well as England. In 1694, William ordered the construction of the chief royal yacht of his reign, the 152-ton *William and Mary*, built at Chatham by Surveyor R. Lee. It had a length on the gundeck of 76 feet 6 inches, a length at the keel of 61 feet 5 inches, a beam of 21 feet 7 inches, a depth in the hold of 9 feet 6 inches, was single-masted, ketch-rigged and armed with eight three-pounder guns. It was named after themselves as King and Queen. It frequently conveyed William III, or his military officers and government staff, or both, to Holland when crises occurred there.

In 1697, Tsar Peter the Great of Russia toured western Europe and, in particular, the maritime nations. He was nautically minded, with the aim of increasing the size and quality of his own navy. He even worked as a carpenter at the Zaandam shipyard in Holland for six months. He had stated his intention to visit England and so William III sent HMS *Yorke* to fetch the Tsar from Holland. On reaching the Thames Estuary, he was transferred to the royal yacht *William and Mary* and, escorted by other royal yachts, sailed on it to London Bridge to disembark for Whitehall.

Tsar Peter soon became bored with the tedium of daily court life and so quickly moved in with the scientist and diarist John Evelyn at the latter's home, Sayes Court, so he was able to work and study in the nearby Deptford Dockyard. William III shrewdly decided to take advantage of this situation to cultivate trade with Russia and ordered a ship to be built at Deptford as a gift to Tsar Peter and on which the Tsar himself almost certainly worked. Known as *Royal Transport* and not named after the Tsar as might have been expected, it was designed by Peregrine, Lord Danby, a friend of the Tsar. In May 1698, it sailed for Holland with Tsar Peter on his own royal yacht.

An alternative version of this account states that, after the Tsar made known his wish to visit England and some of its dockyards, William III sent his own royal yacht, *Transport Royal*, to Holland to collect the Tsar. The Tsar was reputedly highly delighted by this and is supposed to have sailed *Transport Royal* across the North Sea to the Thames Estuary where he transferred to a royal barge to be rowed upriver, past the Tower of London and London Bridge to Whitehall. I have, however, been unable to ascertain the existence of such a vessel as the *Transport Royal*.

William III was persuaded to build a ship of the class of the *Royal Transport* for his own Navy. In 1700, the 197-ton *Peregrine Galley*, also designed by Peregrine, Lord Danby, was built at Sheerness by Surveyor R. Lee. It had a length on the gundeck of 86 feet 10 inches, a length at the keel of 72 feet 8 inches, a beam of 22 feet, a depth in the hold of 10 feet 7 inches, and was armed with twenty cannon and twelve swivel guns. From naval service as a sixth rate, it was refitted in 1716 as a royal yacht and renamed *Carolina* after Caroline of Anspach, the future Queen of George II. In 1733, it was again renamed as *Royal Caroline* when rebuilt. In 1749, it was renamed yet again when it was converted to a sloop (a single-masted, fore-and-aft rigged ship, with jib, mainsail, staysail and gaff topsail) warship, finally being sunk in the Bay of Biscay in 1762. It used to be a superstition of dread among seafarers that renaming a ship after its launch was asking for misfortune. They would claim it did so with the *Peregrine Galley*.

Several other small yachts were built during the reign of William and Mary, but for naval or official service, not especially for the use of the monarchs. The 37-ton *Squirrel* (*Squirrill*) was built at Chatham in 1694 by Surveyor R. Lee. It had a length at the keel of 36 feet, a beam of 14 feet, a depth in the hold of 6 feet and was armed with four two-pounder guns. The reason for the name is unknown. It was used as a service yacht at Chatham Dockyard until sold off in

1714. The 38-ton *Scout* was built at Portsmouth in 1695 by Surveyor R. Stigant. It had a length at the keel of 38 feet 6 inches, a beam of 13 feet 8 inches, a depth in the hold of 6 feet, but its armament is uncertain, probably four two-pounder guns. Again the reason for the name is unknown. It was used as a service yacht in Portsmouth Dockyard until sold off in 1703. The 44-ton *Queenborough* (II) was built at Deptford in 1701 by Surveyor N. Lee. Its dimensions are not recorded. It was also named after Queenborough, Isle of Sheppey, Kent, and retained in Sheerness Dockyard, but its use is unknown.

The Isle of Wight (II) was the original 30-ton *Isle of Wight* built Portsmouth 1673, but rebuilt in Portsmouth, in 1701, by Surveyor 'Mr. Wasse'. The tonnage increased from 30 to 38 tons, it was lengthened by 3 feet at the keel to 36 feet 9 inches, the beam increased to 14 feet, the depth in the hold stayed the same and it was armed with four three-pounder guns. It was named after its predecessor. When rebuilt it was used in the service of the Governor of the Isle of Wight, but this was one of the royal yachts that in wartime had its armament increased to be used in the Royal Navy, usually in the English Channel, Thames and Medway Estuaries. It was sold off in 1712.

The *Fubbs* (II) was the original 148-ton *Fubbs*, built in Greenwich, in 1682, and rebuilt in Woolwich, in 1701 by Surveyor N. Lee. The tonnage was increased from 148 to 157 tons, the length at the keel shortened by 2 feet to 61 feet, the beam increased from 21 feet to 22 feet, the depth in the hold stayed the same, it remained single-masted and ketch-rigged, and its armament also stayed the same. And then there was the mysterious royal yacht, *Princess Mary* cum *Betsey Cairns*, as it was referred to in the *New York Times* on 11 March 1883. I include the report as published to allow readers to judge for themselves:

Princess Mary alias *Betsey Cairns* – This ship, according to reliable accounts, was built on the Thames in the earlier part of the seventeenth century and was purchased by the Prince of Orange and selected by the Prince to convey himself and his suite to England. He bestowed upon her the name of the *Princess Mary* in honor of his royal and illustrious Consort, the daughter of James II. During the whole of William's reign, the ship held a place of honor as one of the royal yachts and was often used as the pleasure yacht of Queen Anne. The vessel came in to the possession of George I, by whose order she ceased to form part of the royal establishment and about the middle of the last century was sold to Messrs Walters of London, from whom she received the name *Betsey Cairns* in honor, as we are told, of a West India lady. Afer that she was alternately a West Indiaman, a privateer, a Smyrna figger and a Baltic trader, in all of which capacities she acquitted herself for steadiness, comfort and speed. Various fortunes attended her for many years, until at length she again got into the royal service as a transport under George III and was employed in 1810 at the siege of Cadiz, where she was the headquarters of the marine artillery. With the piping times of peace the *Betsey Cairns* resumed her mercantile avocations and at length, after manifold degradations, having been purchased by Mr. George French Wilson of Shields, she was reduced to the drudgery of carrying coals from Newcastle to London. Here was a descent from a royal yacht to a dowdy collier. In this deplorable condition she lingered on until the 17th of February, 1827, when, while pursuing her voyage from Shields to Hamburg with a cargo of coal she struck upon the "Black Middens", a dangerous reef of rocks to the north of the mouth of the Tyne and in a few days became a total wreck. Thus perished one of the most remarkable ships in the world, after having been constantly at sea for a period of 150 years. She had been regarded with an almost superstitious feeling of interest and veneration and a memorable prophecy was associated with her fortunes, viz., "that the Catholics would never get the better while the *Betsey Cairns* was afloat". The remnant of her original timbering was extremely fine. It was loaded with a profusion of rich and elaborate oak carvings, the color of the wood, from age and exposure, closely resembling that of ebony. Snuff-boxes and souvenirs of various kinds were made of the wood and brought extravagant prices. Each of the members of the then Corporation of Newcastle was presented with one of these boxes of old British oak. The Hon. Stephen Lushington, DCL, one of the most celebrated jurists in Great Britain, in 1856 stated in the British Admiralty Court that in 1816 he was counsel in a cause relating to this ship. When William III landed at Torbay the *Princess Mary* bore a flag with English colors and their highnesses' arms surrounded with the motto "The Protestant Religion and the Liberties of England" and underneath the motto of the House of Nassau, "Je maintiendrai" (I Will Maintain). William wished to land on the 4th of November, the day on which he was born and married, but by the advice of his counselors was persuaded to land the next day, that being the anniversary of the Gunpowder Plot and the celebration of the Protestant religion in England. The *Princess Mary* was more than half a century old when William landed from her at Torbay, Nov 5th, 1688. She was 80 feet 3 inches long, 23 feet broad, double-decked, with two masts, square-rigged. Her earlier name is said to have been *Brill* but this, we believe, is not established. – Rear Admiral G. H. Preble, in the United Service.

Paymaster Commander Gavin in his *Royal Yachts* states: 'William the Third landed at Tor Bay in the autumn of 1688 in the *Brill* or *Briel*, a frigate attached to the fleet sent to bring him to England. The following spring the *Mary* yacht with others was sent with the fleet to escort Queen Mary to England. The Queen landed at Greenwich on February the 12th, 1689. It was at one time believed these services were carried out by a Royal yacht named the *Princess Mary*. Actually there was never any Royal yacht so-called, but there was a vessel of that name which afterwards became the famous *Betsy Cains*.' He then relates the latter's career and fate, and concludes with: 'In the London Index 1786 there is an entry giving the name *Princess Mary* and captured that year. The *Betsy Cains* first appears in the Lloyds Register of Shipping in 1802, built 1690, wrecked 1827. There is no evidence to show a vessel of either of those names was at any time a Royal Yacht.'

Queen Anne (1702–14), second daughter of James II, was not so keen on sailing as to become an enthusiastic seafarer, but in addition to the fifteen royal yachts she inherited, several more were built. One was the 104-ton *Isabella* (II) built Deptford 1703 by Surveyor 'Mr Harding'. Its details and dimensions were unrecorded, except that the armament was eight three-pounder guns. It was sold off in 1715.

The *Charlot* (II) was the original 143-ton *Charlot* that was built at Woolwich in 1677 and rebuilt at Deptford in 1710, by Surveyor Joshua Allin, Snr. The tonnage was increased from 143 to 155 tons, the length at the keel reduced from 61 feet 9 inches to 57 feet 7 inches, the beam increased from 20 feet 6 inches to 22 feet 6 inches, the depth in the hold was 9 feet 6 inches, it was single-masted, but yacht-rigged, and its armament remained the same. In the reign of George II, 1736, it was ketch-rigged, lengthened to 79 feet in 1747, and in George III's reign, 1761, renamed *Augusta*.

Previous to *Charlot* (II), Queen Anne had ordered the building of another *Portsmouth*. The new example of 66 tons was built at Portsmouth in 1702 by

Surveyor Thomas Podd. It had a length on the gundeck of 52 feet 10 inches, a length at the keel of 42 feet 10 inches, a beam of 17 feet, a depth in the hold of 8 feet and was armed with six two-pounder guns. It was named after the port, being used at first in the service of the Commissioner of Portsmouth Dockyard. In the reign of George II, 1741, it was renamed *Old Portsmouth* and in 1752 was refitted for the use of the young gentlemen at the Portsmouth Naval Academy. In 1772, in the reign of George III, it was repaired and refitted for the service of the Governor of the Isle of Wight and renamed *Medina* after the River Medina on the island, being broken up in the reign of William IV, 1832.

The *Portsmouth* (II) was followed by the 50-ton *Drake*, built in Portsmouth in 1705 by Surveyor 'Mr. Locke'. It had a length at the keel of 34 feet 9 inches, a beam of 16 feet 6 inches, a depth in the hold of 9 feet and was armed with six three-pounder guns. It was first used in the service of the Commissioner of Plymouth Dockyard. Four years later in 1709, the 42-ton *Bolton* was built at Portsmouth by Surveyor Thomas Todd. It had a length on the gundeck of 53 feet, a length at the keel of 38 feet, a beam of 14 feet 6 inches, a depth in the hold of 7 feet 6 inches and was armed with six two-pounder guns. It was named after the Duke of Bolton, Lord Lieutenant of Hampshire, and used in his service as Governor of the Isle of Wight. In the reign of George III, 1763, *Bolton* was also refitted for the use of the young gentlemen at Portsmouth Naval Academy, until broken up 1817. Also, in 1709, the 148-ton *Dublin* was built at Deptford by Surveyor Joshua Allin. It had a length on the gundeck of 73 feet, a length at the keel of 59 feet 8 inches, a beam of 21 feet 7 inches, was ketch-rigged and armed with ten three-pounder guns. Due to its name, not surprisingly, it was used in the service of the Lord Lieutenant of Ireland.

In the eighteenth and nineteenth centuries, from 1714 to 1830, the several King Georges – I, II, III and IV – were all also Electors of Hanover in Germany and had estates there with which they had to maintain contact. This meant that they had to travel to Europe by sea and required royal yachts for official use as well as pleasure.

George I (1714–27) inherited fifteen royal yachts of varying ages and sizes built in earlier reigns, some of which were sold off during his reign. He was only interested in them as a means of transporting himself to and from Europe. In 1716, the *Peregrine Galley*, built in the reign of William III, was refitted at Deptford as the principal royal yacht. Its upperworks were changed to make it the first royal yacht to be ship-rigged and it was renamed *Carolina* in honour of Carolina of Anspach-Brandenburg, the wife of the future George II. In the reign of George II (1727–60), it was rebuilt in 1733 and renamed *Royal Caroline*.

In 1716, the 60-ton *Chatham* was built at Chatham by Surveyor Mr Rotwill. It had a length on the gundeck of 56 feet, a length at the keel of 44 feet 6 inches, a beam of 16 feet, a depth in the hold of 7 feet 6 inches and was armed with four two-pounder guns. It was named after where it was to be based, in the service of the Commissioner of Chatham Dockyard, and sold off in the reign of George II, 1742.

This account of the royal yachts now reaches a period when the frequent duplication and triplication of some of the earlier names occurs and can be confusing. This is usually due to the earlier examples being rebuilt, taken apart, extended, shortened, heightened, strengthened, etc.

The *Katherine* (III), built at Chatham as *Katherine* (II) in 1674, was rebuilt at Deptford in 1720 as the 161-ton *Katherine* (III) by Surveyor R. Stacey. Its dimensions were altered to give a length on the gundeck of 76 feet 6 inches, a length at the keel of 61 feet six inches, a beam of 22 feet 4 inches, a depth in the hold of 9 feet 6 inches and an armament of eight three-pounder guns. It was refitted as a ketch in the reign of George II, 1736, and sold off in the reign of George III, 1801. One of the important tasks of *Katherine* (III) was to convey Princess Caroline, daughter of George III, to Holland en route to her marriage to King Christian VII of Denmark.

Another repeat name is *Fubbs* (III), built at Greenwich as *Fubbs* (I) in 1682, rebuilt at Woolwich in 1701 as *Fubbs* (II), and rebuilt again at Deptford in 1724 as the 152-ton *Fubbs* (III), by Surveyor R. Stacey. Its dimensions were altered to a gundeck of 76 feet 9 inches, a length at the keel 61 feet 6 inches, a beam of 21 feet 6 inches, a depth in the hold 9 feet and an armament of eight three-pounder guns. In the reign of George II, 1749, the deck was raised; the royal yacht being broken up in the reign of George III, 1781

The *Mary* (III) was built at Chatham in 1677 as *Mary* (II), but rebuilt in Deptford in 1727 as the 164-ton *Mary* (III) by Surveyor R. Stacey. Its dimensions were altered to a length at the keel of 61 feet 6 inches, a beam of 22 feet 4 inches, a depth in the hold of 9 feet 8 inches and an armament of eight three-pounder guns and ten swivel guns. In the reign of George II, 1735, it was re-rigged as a ketch and in the reign of George III re-rigged again, being broken up in 1816. It was named after its predecessor *Mary* (II), probably after Mary, daughter of James II, later Queen of England.

The 44-ton *Queenborough* (II), built at Deptford in 1701, was rebuilt at Sheerness in 1718 as the 46-ton *Queenborough* (III) by Surveyor John Ward. It had a length on the gundeck of 51 feet, a length at the keel of 37 feet 3 inches, a beam of 15 feet, a depth in the hold of 6 feet 6 inches and was armed with six two-pounder guns. Named after its predecessor, it was used in the service of the Commissioner of Sheerness Dockyard until the reign of George III, when it was refitted as a survey vessel in 1775 and based at Sheerness until sold off in 1777.

George II (1727–60) inherited six royal yachts from previous reigns, but, like his father George I, was not overly enthusiastic about the sea and voyaging on it, though he too had to return frequently to Hanover on royal duty. The *Peregrine Galley* built at Sheerness in 1700 was refitted as a royal yacht and renamed *Carolina* in 1716, and during George II's reign was rebuilt at Deptford in 1733 by Surveyor 'Mr Stacey' and renamed the 216-ton *Royal Caroline*. Its dimensions were altered to a length of 86 feet 6 inches on the gundeck, a length at the keel of 70 feet 6 inches, a beam of 24 feet, a depth in the hold of 10 feet 6 inches and an armament of ten three-pounder guns. In 1749, it was rebuilt as a sloop and renamed *Peregrine Sloop*, but was lost with all on board on a voyage to the West Indies in 1762. The Lords of the Admiralty decided to build a replacement royal yacht, *Royal Caroline* (II). This vessel, named after its predecessor, was 232 tons and built at Deptford in 1749 by Surveyor Joshua Allin. It had a length on the gundeck of 90 feet, a length at the keel of 72 feet 2 inches, a beam of 24 feet 7 inches, a depth in the hold of 11 feet and was armed with ten three-pounder guns and eight half-pounder swivel guns. During the reign of George III, however, it was renamed *Royal Charlotte* in 1761 and broken up in 1820. In April 1750, three months after the launching of the *Royal Caroline* (II), George II was conveyed from Harwich to Helvoetsluys, Holland, en route to Hanover.

Not surprisingly, because of the high responsibility and importance surrounding the safe transporting of the King and Queen, their family, officers of state, ambassadors and similar notable people, the commands of the royal yachts were in the hands of responsible people who had a lot of wide-ranging experiences and common sense gained from a seafaring life involving varied circumstances on a variety of ships. In the early royal yacht commands, this was usually a reliable and close relative of the monarch. In later centuries, it was sometimes a member of the aristocracy, close to the monarchy, who had had a life at sea, sometimes on the monarch's behalf – but not always. There were instances when the command went to someone who had improved himself by training and experience in his seagoing career. In St Peter and St Paul's church at Shadoxhurst, Kent, is a memorial to one such man.

On the north wall of the chancel is a magnificent white marble monument to the memory of Sir Charles Molloy. Standing alongside his bust is a large weeping figure of a boy, around them being emblems of war. The inscription below states:

> Sir Charles Molloy, Knt. Lord of this Manor, late Captain of His Majesty's ship *Royal Caroline*, some-time a Director of Greenwich Hospital, an Elder Brother of Trinity House and one of His Majesty's Justices of the Peace for the County of Kent ... after a long and faithful service of near sixty years in the Royal Navy where he went very young; with King William's Letter ... He gradually rose and was promoted to the rank of Lieutenant, after the hard-fought Battle of Malaga in the Mediterranean with the French fleet in the year 1704 (being then in the *Royal Oak* which had a large share in that day's action) in which post he continued till the year 1714 when he was by the Earl of Berkeley (who then commanded the Fleet) appointed Captain of His Majesty's yatch the *William and Mary* in which and afterwards in the *May* yatch he served until the seventh day of April, 1742, when His Majesty King George the Second by his especial command was pleased to appoint him his own captain in the *Royal Caroline* and afterwards, in a voyage Royal of his being bound for Holland on the twenty-seventh day of April, 1743 (His Majesty then being on board at Gravesend) and the Royal Standard hoisted he was pleased as a further mark of his royal favour to confer upon him the honour of knighthood and in all of which employs he ever discharged his duty as became an officer and seaman, he was twice married ... He left no issue and departed this life August the 24th, 1760, aged 76. Dame Ellen Molloy who departed this life the 15th of October, 1765, aged 54 years, (second wife).

Molloy's box tomb with iron railings is in the churchyard close to the north-east corner of the church chancel. It appears badly in need of restoration.

Like its predecessor *Drake* (I), built in Plymouth by Surveyor 'Mr. Locke', 1705, it was rebuilt in Plymouth, in 1729, as the 68-ton *Drake* (II), also by 'Mr Locke'. It is assumed it was named after Sir Francis Drake, especially as it was used as a yacht in the service of the Commissioner for Plymouth Dockyard until sold off in 1749. Its dimensions on rebuilding were altered to a length at the keel of 45 feet and its armament changed to six two-pounder guns.

Also named after its predecessor was *Chatham* (II), built at Chatham in 1716 as the 60-ton *Chatham I*, it was rebuilt there in 1741 as the 74-ton *Chatham* (II), designed and built by Surveyor John Ward. Its dimensions were altered to a length on the gundeck of 59 feet 6 inches, a length at the keel of 47 feet, a beam of 17 feet 3 inches, a depth in the hold the same and an armament of six two-pounder guns. It was used as a yacht in the service of the Commissioner for Chatham Dockyard, being rebuilt again in the reign of George III, 1793.

The third royal yacht with the name of *Portsmouth* was the 83-ton *Portsmouth* (III), designed and built by Surveyor P. Locke at Portsmouth in 1742. It had a length on the gundeck of 59 feet 6 inches, a length at the keel of 48 feet 5 inches, a beam of 18 feet, a depth in the hold of 8 feet 6 inches and was armed with six two-pounder guns. It was used as a yacht in the service of the Commissioner of Portsmouth Dockyard, being rebuilt in the reign of George III, 1794.

The reason for naming a royal yacht *Dorset* is unknown, especially as it was used elsewhere. The 164-ton vessel was built at Deptford in 1753 by Sir T. Slade. It had a length of the gundeck of 78 feet, length at the keel of 64 feet 10 inches, a beam of 21 feet 11 inches, a depth in the hold of 10 feet 10 inches, was ketch rigged, but later three-masted, and armed with six two-pounder guns and fourteen half-pounder swivel guns. It was used as a yacht in the service of the Lord Lieutenant of Ireland and based at Dublin until broken up in the reign of George III, 1815.

The 88-ton *Plymouth* was named after the port and town in which it was designed and built by a Thomas Bucknoll in 1755. It had a length on the gundeck of 64 feet 6 inches, a length at the keel of 52 feet 6 inches, a beam of 17 feet 10 inches, a depth in the hold of 10 feet and was armed with six two-pounder guns. It was used as a yacht in the service of the Commissioner of Plymouth Dockyard until broken up in the reign of George III, 1793.

George III (1760–1820) inherited eighteen royal yachts of former reigns, some of them for his and Royal Family use, others for varied naval service. A new example, the 278-ton *Royal Sovereign*, was built at Deptford in 1804 and designed by Sir John Henslow. It had a length on the gundeck of 96 feet, a length at the keel of 80 feet 5 inches, a beam of 25 feet 6 inches, a depth in the hold of 10 feet and was armed with eight three-pounder guns.

In 1814, King Louis XVIII returned to France from his long exile in England, following Napoleon Bonaparte's imprisonment on Elba. The royal yacht, *Royal Sovereign*, took part in this royal event. After the Prince Regent had invested Louis with the Order of the Garter, he travelled with him from London to Dover and there, on 24 April, Louis embarked on the *Royal Sovereign* and was waved off by the Prince. The royal yacht was escorted by a thirty-two-gun frigate, *Jason*, and the French frigate *Polonais*. On board the *Jason* was William, Duke of Clarence (later William IV) and Admiral of the Fleet. On arriving at Calais several hours later, the *Royal Sovereign* hove to as the Duke, on the *Jason*, sailed past the royal yacht and the ship's crew manned the yard arms and gave three rousing cheers. After this the *Royal Sovereign* put into Calais to disembark Louis XVIII, and the Duke of Clarence transferred from *Jason* to the warship *Impregnable* to welcome aboard Tsar Alexander I of Russia, King Frederick William III of Prussia and Prince Metternich of Austria, who were to be conveyed from Calais to Portsmouth and eventually to London to attend the celebration of Napoleon's downfall. The Duke of Clarence was in command of the *Royal Sovereign* and others in the escorting fleet.

In 1827, William, Duke of Clarence, was appointed Lord High Admiral whereon the flag for this office bearing the red and gold anchor was broken on the foremast of the *Royal Sovereign* and, with Duke William aboard, it sailed up the Channel into the North Sea for one of his numerous 'cruises', to the dismay of the Lords of the Admiralty, to escape protocol for several days. The *Royal Sovereign* was converted to a depot ship at Pembroke Dockyard in 1832 and finally broken up in 1850.

Like some of his forebears, George III also used his royal yacht for a matrimonial purpose. He was to marry Charlotte Sophia, Princess of Mecklenburg-Strelitz, but, being a king and his bride a princess, she had to come to him to be married. To honour his future bride, he had already had the *Royal Caroline* (II) renamed the *Royal Charlotte*. To complete his marriage, the *Royal Charlotte*, accompanied by five other royal yachts and several of His Majesty's naval ships, sailed from

A model of the 1804 Royal Yacht *Royal Sovereign*. (Mr G. L. Orry, Molkington, Chester)

Harwich on 7 August 1761, en route to Cuxhaven, Lower Saxony, Germany, to embark the Princess Charlotte. Her return was delayed by violent gales at sea, but eventually the *Royal Charlotte* arrived at Harwich on 6 September; the Princess disembarked on 7 September and reached Whitehall the same day, with much relief to all fearful for her safety on the voyage back to England. The *Royal Charlotte* was eventually broken up in 1820.

The *Princess Augusta* was the original 155-ton *Charlot* (II) of 1710, rebuilt and renamed *Augusta* in 1761, and rebuilt again at Deptford in 1771 by a surveyor, name unrecorded, as the 184-ton *Augusta* (II). Its dimensions were 80 feet 6 inches for the length of the gundeck, a length at the keel of 65 feet, a beam of 23 feet, a depth in the hold of 10 feet 11 inches and it was ship-rigged, no longer ketch-rigged, and armed with eight three-pounder guns. It was renamed *Princess Augusta* in 1773 to mark the occasion of the King reviewing the fleet at Portsmouth in that year. George III used it himself as a royal yacht for a review of the fleet off The Nore in 1778 and in the same year, with Queen Charlotte aboard, reviewed the fleet at Spithead.

In March/April 1795, there was another instance of a royal yacht being used to convey a princess from Europe to marry into English royalty. Princess Caroline of Brunswick, bride-to-be of Prince George, later George IV, arrived at Gravesend in HMS *Jupiter* and was then conveyed by royal barge to the *Princess Augusta* for the short trip upriver to Greenwich, to disembark there on 4 April.

The *William and Mary* (II) was originally built at Chatham in 1694 as the 152-ton *William and Mary* (I), being rebuilt at Deptford in 1765 as the 172-ton

William and Mary (II) by Surveyor A. Hayes. The length of the gundeck remained the same in that alteration but the length at the keel was extended to 62 feet 10 inches, with a beam of 22 feet 8 inches, a depth in the hold of 10 feet, and was ketch-rigged and armed with the same guns. In 1785, decay necessitated 'a very large repair'. The *Chatham* (III) was another royal yacht from which value for money originally expended was obtained. Built at Chatham in 1716 as *Chatham* (I) and rebuilt at Chatham in 1741 as the 74-ton *Chatham* (II), it was again rebuilt at Chatham in 1793, as the 90-ton *Chatham* (III), the designer-builder unrecorded. Its dimensions on rebuilding were a similar length on the gundeck, a length at the keel of 47 feet 3 inches, a beam of 18 feet 7 inches, and a depth in the hold of 9 feet 8 inches. Obviously named after its predecessors, it was used as a yacht of the Commissioner of Chatham Dockyard until broken up in 1867. During its career, however, it was to perform a national service that no one could ever have expected it to do, and in fact the nation would have preferred it not to have to do – transporting of the body of Admiral Lord Nelson after his death at the Battle of Trafalgar.

The occasion is described in detail in volume IV of *The Naval History of Great Britain* by William James, published in 1837:

In 1805 the *Chatham* (III) was in service as the Commissioner of Sheerness Dockyard's Yacht, he being the Honourable George Grey. After the Battle of Trafalgar on 25th October the *Victory* was towed into Gibraltar for repairs by the *Neptune*, arriving there on the 28th; having on board preserved in spirits, the body of the late lamented hero, whose flag she had so long borne and which was then flying on board her but in a melancholy position at half-mast. On the arrival of the *Victory* back in England the Admiralty had ordered the *Chatham* (III) to attend the *Victory* and take on board it the coffin containing Lord Nelson then to continue to Greenwich with this on board. On 23 December the event detailed in the Log of the *Victory* stated: "At 1.40 shortened sail and anchored with the small bower (anchor) in 12 fm in The Swin. Moored ship. Came alongside Commissioner Grey's yacht from Sheerness and rec'd the remains of the late Lord Viscount Nelson KB and Vice-Admiral of the White. Got a pilot on board to take the ship (*Victory*) to Chatham."

How ironic that the *Victory*, built at Chatham and part of the great naval victory and also the site of Nelson's demise, returned to the dockyard where it originated. Prior to *Chatham* (III) arriving, Nelson's body had been taken out of the spirits cask and placed in a coffin made by the ship's carpenters using timber from a wrecked ship that had been with Nelson at the Battle of the Nile. The wood coffin was then put into a lead coffin and the latter sealed with solder to make it airtight and watertight. This was then lowered from the *Victory* to the *Chatham* (III), the latter bearing Nelson's flag half-mast.

The account in *The Naval History of Great Britain* concludes: 'On the 24th, at 2 p.m. the yacht, having in the passage up had military honours paid to her illustrious charge on both sides of the river anchored off Greenwich and at 7 p.m. the body was landed at the centre gate of the Royal Hospital, amidst an immense crowd of spectators. The aweful and imposing ceremony which subsequently took place having been minutely detailed by other publications we shall content ourselves with stating that on the 9th January, 1806, this first of naval captains was buried in St. Paul's cathedral, with all the pomp and solemnity befitting the occasion.'

The fourth royal yacht with the name of *Portsmouth* was the 102-ton *Portsmouth* (IV), originally built at Portsmouth in 1742 as the 83-ton *Portsmouth* (III), was rebuilt at Portsmouth in 1794, designed by Surveyor P. Locke. The dimensions in the alterations were: the length of the gundeck to 70 feet 4 inches, a length at the keel of 53 feet 9 inches, a beam of 18 feet 11 inches, a depth in the hold of 11 feet 8 inches, and an armament of six two-pounder guns. It was used as a yacht in the service of the Commissioner of Portsmouth Dockyard until broken up in the reign of Queen Victoria, 1869.

The second royal yacht named *Plymouth,* after the city, was the 96-ton *Plymouth* (II), built at Plymouth in 1796 to the design of Surveyor Sir John Henslow. The length of the gundeck was 64 feet, the length at the keel was 52 feet 7 inches, it had a beam of 18 feet 6 inches, a depth in the hold of 10 feet 1 inch, and its armament is unrecorded. Named after its predecessor, it was used as a yacht in the service of the Commissioner of Plymouth Dockyard until broken up in 1830.

The third royal yacht with the name of *William and Mary* was the 199-ton *William and Mary* (III), built at Deptford in 1807, designed by Surveyor Sir John Henslow. The dimensions in the alteration were: the length of the gundeck was 85 feet, the length at the keel was 70 feet 3½ inches, and it had a beam of 23 feet and a depth in the hold of 11 feet. It was used as a yacht in the service of the Lord Lieutenant of Ireland at Dublin from 1813 to 1827. From 1832, it was a depot ship in Woolwich Dockyard until broken up 1849.

George III had the physical misfortune to suffer reputedly from the effects of porphyria, an inborn disorder of the metabolism that periodically caused him to appear insane, therefore his son George, Prince of Wales, ruled as Prince Regent from 1811 to 1820, being king in all but name. He inherited some of the royal yachts from his father and earlier monarchs, four of these were sold during the Regency. However, he followed previous Georges by ordering the construction of three more, two named after himself. They were the *Royal George, Prince Regent* and *Royal Charlotte* (II).

The 330-ton *Royal George,* designed by Surveyor Sir Henry Peake, was laid down at Deptford in 1814 and launched in 1817. It had a length on the gundeck of 103 feet, a length at the keel of 88 feet 4 inches, a beam of 26 feet 6 inches, a depth in the hold of 11 feet 6 inches, was three-masted, ship-rigged, and armed with eight swivel one-pounder brass guns. It was, in fact, the first of two royal yachts that the Prince Regent named after himself. Considering the exotic flamboyance of his Pavilion at Brighton, it is not surprising such style was applied to these vessels. Paymaster Commander Gavin, in his *Royal Yachts,* published in 1932, describes the appearance of one of them: 'The vessel is the most elegant ever seen. The cabin doors are mahogany with gilt mouldings and the windows of plate glass. Ornamental devices in abundance are placed in various parts, all highly gilt and producing superb appearance.'

Due to his profligate and licentious lifestyle the Prince Regent was very unpopular with the general population, whereas his badly treated wife, Caroline, was immensely popular. Despite this, large crowds used to gather at Brighthelmstone (Brighton) to see him at his Pavilion and when he set off to sea in the *Royal George* on numerous occasions, cruising up and down the English Channel and around the Isle of Wight. So enthusiastic did he become in regard to his cruising that in 1817 he bought a seafront property at Cowes in order to have a base on the island.

In 1821, the *Royal George* took King George IV to Holyhead, en route to Ireland. However, due to the death of his unhappy wife, Caroline, on 8 August, his journey was disrupted and he did not reach Dublin until 12 August in a steam ship, the *Talbot.* He returned in the *Royal George* to Portsmouth. In September of that year, as Elector of Hanover, similar to his three predecessors, he sailed from Ramsgate to stay in Hanover, where he was popular with the people, until November, when he returned to England and Brighton. The citizens of Ramsgate were so grateful for the 'favour' King George IV had bestowed on their town and port by his 'visit' that they raised a tall obelisk, said to be on the spot where he stepped ashore on his return. The inscription on it reads: 'To George the Fourth, King of Great Britain and Ireland the Inhabitants and Visitors of Ramsgate and the Directors and Trustees of the Harbour Have Erected This Obelisk as a Grateful Record of His Majesty's Gracious Condescension in Selecting This Port for His Embarkaition on the 25th September in progress to His Kingdom of Hanover and His Happy Return on the 8th November, 1821.' George IV changed embarkation venue on 10 August 1822, when he boarded the *Royal George* at Greenwich for a visit to Scotland, anchoring off Leith on 18 August.

The *Royal George* continued in use until the reign of Queen Victoria. It was inherited from her uncle William IV by Queen Victoria, who loved cruising at sea. In 1842, she and Prince Albert sailed in the royal yacht to Leith in Scotland, embarking at Woolwich on 29 August, the *Royal George* having been towed there by two steam ships, accompanied by seven other steam ships, two Royal Navy warships and the Trinity House steamship *Vestal*. It had been a slow and rough voyage of three days. The seasick Queen chartered the paddle steamer *Trident* for the return voyage.

In 1843, *Royal George* became an accommodation ship for the officers and yachtsmen serving on the royal yachts, but in 1902, Edward VII ordered it to be paid off and the officers and yachtsmen to be accommodated on the vessel on which they were serving. In 1905, it was broken up. The hand steering wheel and binnacles of the *Royal George* were later installed in *Victoria and Albert* (III).

The second of George IV's royal yachts was the 282-ton *Prince Regent*, laid down at Portsmouth in 1815, launched in 1820 and designed by the Portsmouth Naval Academy. The length of the gundeck was 96 feet, it had a length at the keel of 81 feet 3 inches, a beam of 25 feet, a depth in the hold of 10 feet, and its armament is unrecorded. It was also the second of two royal yachts correctly named after him, as he was at this time still the Prince Regent. As *Royal George* gave the future King George IV such pleasure when Regent, it seems it continued to do so and the later *Prince Regent* had a lesser role of conveying other royalty and personages of note to and from Europe. One voyage of this kind is referred to in an edition of the *Kentish Gazette* of Canterbury, dated 14 May 1822:

The *Prince Regent* royal yacht sailed from The Downs (a safe anchorage opposite Deal, Kent) on Saturday morning for Calais to take on board the Crown Prince of Denmark but returned again to The Downs on Sunday evening without having had communication with that port. In consequence of the tides preventing an entrance into the harbour and a violent wind from the north-east with a very heavy sea on the coast. As the wind has since become moderate the *Prince Regent* will sail again this morning and His Royal Highness may be expected to reach Dover tomorrow, where His Excellency the Danish Envoy arrived on Sunday to receive him.

Ah, the fickleness of wind and water.

In 1836, *Prince Regent* was taken into Deptford Dockyard for a refit prior to being given as a gift to the Imam of Muscat, Arabia, after which it was reputed to have been broken up in 1847. The third of George IV's royal yachts was the 202-ton *Royal Charlotte* (II), built at Woolwich between 1820 and 1824, and designed by Surveyor R. Seppings. It had a length on the gundeck of 85 feet

The obelisk on the Harbour
Parade, Ramsgate, near the end
of East Pier, commemorating the
arrival and departure of George
IV in 1821, via the Royal Yacht.
(Author)

8 inches, a length at the keel of 72 feet 8 inches, a beam of 23 feet, a depth in the hold of 8 feet 2 inches, and was armed with eight one-pounder swivel guns. It was named after his daughter, Charlotte, by his wife, Princess Caroline of Brunswick, and was the last royal yacht to be used in the service of the Lord Lieutenant of Ireland at Dublin until 1832, when it was broken up at Pembroke Dockyard.

King William IV (1830–37), nicknamed 'The Sailor King', inherited eight various royal yachts from earlier reigns, five of them being sold off in his reign. He built but one new royal yacht, the 50-ton miniature frigate *Royal Adelaide* (I), not for himself but for his children by his mistress, the actress Mrs Jordan. Curiously he named it after his childless wife, Queen Adelaide, sister of the Duke of Saxe-Meiningen. It was built at Sheerness in 1833 by Surveyor Sir William Symonds. The length at the keel was 50 feet with, surprisingly in view of its use, a copper-plated hull bottom, and a beam of 15 feet. Equally surprising, it was 'armed' with twenty-two one-pounder brass guns. When complete it was taken apart and conveyed to Virginia Water in Surrey, where it was reassembled for use on the lake to entertain William's children and later Queen Victoria's children. It was not broken up until 1877.

With the start of Queen Victoria's reign (1837–1901), this narrative enters, from sail-powered royal yachts, into the age of steam power with *Victoria and Albert* (I). This did not mean the days of sail were over, for members of the Royal Family possessed various sailing craft for more personal enjoyment.

Edward VII, when Prince of Wales, bought his first racing yacht, *Dagmar*, in 1866, followed by *Princess* in 1869, *Alexandra* in 1871, *Zenobia* in 1872, *Hildegarde* in 1876, *Formosa* in 1880 and *Aline* in 1882. In *Aline*, Edward took part in a 1,520-mile race to commemorate his mother's golden jubilee. He was regularly an enthusiastic president of regattas at Cowes and other places where similar events were held. These events were popular sporting and social occasions in the yachting season, attended by other European royalty, millionaire industrialists, bankers, socialites and 'theatricals'. Incidentally, there is a reputed 'story' that Edward, when Prince of Wales, was mystified that his mother was so well informed about numbers and identities of his lady guests and others on the royal yachts *Alberta* and, in particular, *Victoria and Albert* (III), which he could sail to and fro in the area without any fears for his safety. He suspected that there was an informant among the ship's officers or crew. However, the explanation was, according to the 'story', simpler. Allegedly, the Queen had a powerful telescope installed at Osborne House, which she used to watch the royal yachts when they sailed from Portsmouth and past the Isle of Wight. After this became known to Edward, so the 'story' goes, the ladies were advised to stay below deck until the yacht was out of telescopic range. However, in 1898, the Queen had another means of keeping tabs on Edward when she 'communicated by Signor Marconi's "wireless system"' from Osborne House, with him on one of the royal yachts. There is no record of his reaction to this advance in the means of shore-to-ship communication.

Edward's paramour, actress Lily Langtry, was not only one of his mistresses and guests on his maritime jaunts; she enjoyed sailing and was more nautically minded than most of them, perhaps due to her early life on Jersey. She hoped to compete with Edward and wanted a yacht of her own. Whether she dared to do this is doubtful. From a friend, Lord Ashburton, Edward bought her a 400-ton yacht, *The White Lady*, as a surprise gift. Lily, after travelling in Europe, arrived at Cherbourg to join a cross-Channel steamer for England. *The White Lady* was anchored in the harbour awaiting her arrival. As Lily boarded to inspect her gift, Edward was also aboard with documentation transferring the yacht to her ownership and a £50,000 cheque for its maintenance and running costs. When that money was used up, Edward paid again, but when king he could either no longer afford this or be seen paying for the running of his mistress's yacht, so the 'arrangement' ended. To raise the income needed to maintain the vessel, Lily chartered it to various people, among them the American millionaire Ogden Coekt, but its eventual fate is unknown. Meanwhile, in 1892, Edward commissioned the design and construction of the 159-ton racing cutter *Britannia* from George L. Watson, an eminent yacht designer (see *Nahlin*). Built by D. and W. Henderson & Co., Glasgow, it was steel framed with pine and elm planking and topsides, the upperparts of the yacht, above water, were cedar, the interior fittings were yellow pine and mahogany, and the accommodation consisted of a saloon, four guest sleeping cabins, a cabin for the captain, sleeping quarters for all thirty crew members, a galley and a pantry. Registered on 19 May 1893, the yacht's dimensions were: overall length 122 feet 6 inches, loadwater line 88 feet, beam 23 feet 7 inches, draught 16 feet 3 inches, mast height 164 feet, boom 91 feet and spinnaker boom 66 feet – originally gaff-topsail cutter rig, later Bermudan rig with sails of 10,384 square feet by Ratsey & Lapthorn.

During its long career, *Britannia* had several sail plans for the circumstances of its racing or cruising. It began in 1893 with the gaff cutter rig, followed by various other rig changes and mast changes, such as the 7-foot lengthening of the mast in 1920, and a telescopic mast until its final Bermudan rig. In 1932, George V presented a mast from a refit to the Royal Alfred Aged Merchant Seamen's Institution (now the Royal Alfred Seafarers Society) for use as a flag mast at their former home in Belvedere, Kent. When this home closed in 1978, the mast was transported from Belvedere to the society's new home at Banstead in Surrey, and used as a flag mast there until this closed in 2001. Although well maintained, the mast showed signs of decay and a decision was taken not to move it to the society's new nursing home – Weston Acres, Banstead – so sadly it was destroyed.

The black hull design of *Britannia* was a new innovation compared to the hull design of other racing yachts; the bow was not designed in the style of the usual clipper or swan bow, which drove through the water, but to skim the water's surface instead. At first the racing fraternity were sceptical, but it proved highly successful and was soon copied. The first race to test *Britannia* was on the River Thames on 25 May 1893 with Edward aboard, and it won. *Britannia* entered thirty-eight races that year, winning twenty of them. In July 1894, it was entered in the Royal Clyde Yacht Club's Fortnight Races. In the 50-mile race, the larger American yacht, *Vigilant*, won by 67 seconds, but *Britannia* still won on points.

In 1889, Kaiser Wilhelm II of Germany paid his first visit to Cowes Regatta, arriving again in 1891 to take part, which he did regularly until 1895. Kaiser Wilhelm competed against his uncle, Prince Edward, on *Britannia*, with his cutter *Meteor* (I) without success. His pride dented, Wilhelm ordered the building of the cutter *Meteor* (II) in 1896, a longer, larger-sailed version of Edward's *Britannia*. The *Meteor* (II) easily outclassed and beat *Britannia*, and all the other yachts that raced against it, to become the most successful racing yacht of the times. Against this determined-to-win-at-all-costs competition from the Kaiser, Edward's interest in racing faded, and he sold *Britannia* in 1897. It had three private owners until Edward re-purchased it in May 1899, but sold it again to Sir Richard Bulkeley in 1900, probably for economic reasons. Surprisingly, Edward, now King Edward VII, bought the cutter back from Sir Richard in 1902, but did not race it. It continued to appear at Cowes Regatta with the King aboard, welcomed by all who witnessed this beautiful craft as it cruised around.

On the death of Edward VII in 1910, George V, another 'Sailor King', inherited it. He had the same fondness for *Britannia* and during his reign he raced or sailed it for pleasure, often in the Solent at Cowes and various other regattas in 1911, 1912 and 1913. In the last year before the outbreak of the First World War, the *Britannia* raced in June and July at the Irish, Welsh and Scottish Regattas, continuing its successful career, winning eight of the thirteen races in which it was entered. The war put an end to yacht racing and *Britannia* was laid up for the duration on the Medina River on the Isle of Wight. In 1920, George V decided to have *Britannia* overhauled, refitted and to race it again. On 12 July, it entered a race in the Clyde Fortnight and won. At Cowes and various other South Coast regattas, against yachts the quality of *Westward* and *Terpsichore*, it continued to win first and other prizes. At the end of 1922, *Britannia* had a complete refit at Cowes and later took part in the 1923 Clyde Regatta. At Cowes in 1930, under the command of Sir Philip Hunloke, the King's Sailing Master, with George V aboard, *Britannia* won its 200th race. It continued to take part in other regattas, but, at the latter end of his life, the King would only be on board when the yacht was competing at Cowes.

George V, in his Will, decreed that *Britannia* was to be offered to his sons, but if they did not want it to continue racing or cruising, it was to be sunk at sea. According to Angela Fitzroy, the reputed reason for this course of action was to avoid the ignominy of this much-loved yacht entering a breaker's yard, with all that it entailed. However, much of the yacht and its contents were removed prior to the fatal deed. The 175-foot mast was sent to Britannia Royal Naval College; the 50-foot boom went to Carisbrooke Castle, Isle of Wight, to be used as a flag staff. The wheel, compass and various items of gear were sold at auction, raising £1,025, which appropriately went to the King George V Fund for Sailors. On completion of the removals, the solitary black hull was taken from its Cowes slipway to a buoy in the Cowes Roads.

In *Annals of our Royal Yachts, 1604–1952*, by J. E. Grigsby, on page 59 is the King's Steward, Mr Fred Mason's account of what took place there:

At midnight on 9 July (1936) they came for her – two destroyers out of Portsmouth Harbour (H.M. *Amazon* and H.M. *Winchelsea*). On board of them was a handful of men who had loved and served her. There was Sir Philip Hunloke, the late king's Sailing Master, Captain Turner, her skipper, Mr. Fred Mason, the King's Steward and an old pensioner from Portsmouth Dockyard. They towed her round St. Catherine's Point into the deep water and then they pulled her up alongside one of the destroyers. A party went on board and put the explosive down below. They returned to the destroyer and the two ships backed and waited. It was very early morning and as the charge went off those on board the destroyers could just see some pieces fly into the air. They watched for a matter of four or five minutes until the entire hull had disappeared beneath the dark water. They turned the searchlight on her but there was nothing there and the destroyers returned to Portsmouth in the dawn. We were a very sad party.

There was a proposal some years ago to salvage the remains of the hull of *Britannia*, but nothing more was heard of this and it was assumed to have been quietly forgotten in view of the late king's last wishes. It is only right and fitting that *Britannia* should lie secure in the element on which it was so successful.

The 63-foot Flying Fifteen-class racing yacht *Bloodhound*, built in 1936, was used by the Royal Family for pleasure cruising. It was also the royal yacht that Prince Charles, Prince of Wales, and Princess Anne, Princess Royal, learned to sail. It was sold into private ownership in 1969. Another example was the 20-foot Flying Fifteen-class racing yacht *Coweslip*, designed and built in 1947 at Cowes by Uffa Fox, and given to Princess Elizabeth and Prince Philip by the people of Cowes as a gift to mark their wedding. Similarly, the 29-foot Dragon-class *Bluebottle* was a gift to the couple from the Isle of Wight Island Sailing Club.

At this stage in the story of the 'official' royal yachts comes the innovation of steam power. This meant a new concept for these ships, allowing a more reliable and luxurious means of transporting royalty to far-away places, beyond the distances achievable by sail-powered vessels.

The *Queen Elizabeth* and HRH the Duke of Edinburgh's Yacht *Bluebottle*. (J & C McCutcheon Collection)

STEAM TO OBLIVION

The first royal yacht propelled by steam power was *Victoria and Albert* (I). Its keel was laid at Pembroke Dockyard on 9 November 1842, and it was designed and built by Rear-Admiral Sir William Symonds. The ship had an oak and larch wood hull, was two-masted with sails, single-funnelled and paddle-wheeled. Dimensions for the *Victoria and Albert* (I) were: length between perpendiculars (at right angles to the plane of the horizon) was 200 feet 1 inch and its extreme length was 225 feet; the beam (the extreme breadth of this ship at its widest part) was 33 feet; and the draught was 14 feet and its displacement was 1,034 tons. The double-cylinder, direct-acting, paddle-oscillating engines, providing 420 horsepower at a speed of 11.5 knots, were built by Maudslay Sons & Field, Lambeth.

Victoria and Albert (I) was launched at Pembroke on 26 April 1843 by the Countess of Cawdor. On 17 June, Queen Victoria's husband, Prince Albert, with Lords of the Admiralty, visited the ship moored in the Thames. It was commissioned on 1 July and commanded by Captain Lord Adolphus FitzClarence. While the ship was being painted at Deptford, Queen Victoria had also visited it. Afterwards she excitedly wrote in her Journal on 8 August: 'We drove from Woolwich to the Deptford Dockyard where we inspected the *Victoria and Albert* which is a beautiful vessel with splendid accommodation.'

For the Queen's comfort the State Apartments were, not surprisingly, at the rear of the engine room. The accommodation for officers and crew, also the Queen's Suite, were forward in the ship. On the starboard side was the Queen's bedroom, adjoining Prince Albert's dressing room. Nearby were cabins for the royal servants. On the port side was the 25-foot-long, 13-foot-wide, lilac-painted drawing room. Right, aft, was a reception room with a dark-brown patterned carpet, greenish painted walls, furnished with green leather and wood sofas made in the shape to follow the curving contour of the ship's stern.

On its maiden voyage on 28 August 1843, *Victoria and Albert* (I) left Southampton with Queen Victoria and Prince Albert and sailed to Ryde on the Isle of Wight. The weather was unfavourable with grimly dark clouds and a heavy mist. Even so, Queen Victoria wrote on 29 August to her uncle, King of the Belgians, saying, among other comments about the voyage: 'We had not even thought of being sick.' But in her Journal she confided: 'Toward one it got very rough and we both began to feel very uncomfortable so we went below – considering how rough the sea was I must say, the ship was very steady.'

From Ryde, on the maiden voyage, they visited Weymouth, Dartmouth and Plymouth, and then went on to Falmouth where, as had been the case at the other ports the ship had visited, the Mayor and Corporation, officially garbed and wearing their regalia, came aboard to read a Loyal Address to Her Majesty and others assembled to hear it. However, at Falmouth the mayor's dignity was dampened by falling overboard, although luckily he was immediately hauled back onto the yacht. From Falmouth on 2 September, the royal yacht crossed the English Channel and anchored off Tréport, where King Louis Philippe came on board to greet the Queen and Prince Albert. Greetings having been exchanged, both monarchs were rowed ashore in the French king's royal barge to stay at the Chateau d'Eu, one of King Louis Philippe's residences. On 7 September, they took leave of the French king and embarked on *Victoria and Albert* (I) and sailed to Brighton to spend several days with their children. However, the maiden voyage was not over as the royal couple re-embarked and sailed to Ostend to meet Victoria's aunt and uncle, King and Queen of the Belgians, then on to Antwerp, returning to Portsmouth on 21 September. The maiden voyage was considered to be a triumphant success by all concerned with it.

In 1844, the royal couple embarked on *Victoria and Albert* (I) at Woolwich and sailed to Dundee, Scotland, returning three weeks later to Woolwich. In October that same year, on the same yacht, Queen Victoria reviewed the ships of the British and French fleets off Portsmouth. On 15 October, with Prince Albert, the Queen sailed to Ryde, Isle of Wight, to stay at Osborne House, which they had leased and later purchased in 1845 as their rural retreat house. On *Victoria and Albert* (I) at Spithead in June 1845, the Queen reviewed the departure of the Royal Navy's Experimental Squadron comprising of eight battleships of various design that were going to sea to test their success or failings. The same year, the royal couple went on the royal yacht from Woolwich to Germany for Queen Victoria to visit Prince Albert's birthplace, Rosenau Castle, near Coburg. Back in England in

Arrival of the steam yacht *Victoria and Albert* (I) at Tréport, 2 September 1843. (J & C McCutcheon Collection)

September, they once again sailed on *Victoria and Albert* (I) to Tréport in France, to visit King Louis Philippe.

The yacht had immediately proved its worth with these numerous visits to European and United Kingdom ports for sundry purposes of state. During each year, it was also used by the Queen and members of the Royal Family for purposes of pleasure, sailing from port to port, island to island. In 1846, *Victoria and Albert* (I) voyages included Weymouth to Plymouth, Falmouth to Penzance and across to the Channel Islands; in 1847, it voyaged from Dartmouth to the Scilly Isles, to Holyhead and Scotland's West Coast; in 1848, it sailed from Woolwich to Aberdeen, en route to Balmoral; and in August 1849, it sailed to Cork in Ireland for the Queen's first visit to that country, and then on to cruise the Scottish Coast.

In 1850, the royal yacht steamed across the English Channel to Ostend, then on a voyage without royalty to Lisbon and Gibraltar, to see how it fared on longer voyages. It coped, but was not used again for long trips. In 1851, it just visited Liverpool; in 1852, it travelled to various Channel ports, including Antwerp, Belgium; and in 1853, it sailed to Holyhead and then on to Kingstown, Ireland. The *Victoria and Albert* (I), with the Queen aboard, was present on 11 August 1853 at Spithead for her to review ships of the Royal Navy. This was followed by an 'entertainment', which took the form of the royal yacht leading a procession of ships out to sea where a sham fight took place, after which the vessels returned speedily to Spithead for further 'entertainments'.

In 1854, the yacht made a visit to Alderney in the Channel Islands, then to Portland, and then to Boulogne, France. By this time the *Victoria and Albert* (I) was beginning to show its age. It had conveyed Queen Victoria and Prince Albert on twenty voyages to parts of the United Kingdom and Europe. Apart from suffering from a few minor bouts of seasickness, that were not the ship's fault, it seems the Queen was pleased with the performance of this royal yacht. However, taking the ship's age into consideration, a replacement was planned, eventually to be the *Victoria and Albert* (II), laid down at Pembroke in 1854 and launched in 1855. The *Victoria and Albert* (I) was then renamed *Osborne* (I), because it was thought undesirable to have two royal yachts called *Victoria and Albert* at the same time. The *Osborne* (I) still served on secondary royal duties, such as being loaned to the Empress of Austria for a voyage to Madeira, where she was to spend the winter. The *Osborne* (I) was paid off in 1859. The Queen was very reluctant to allow the destruction of the ship on which she had spent so many happy hours with her husband, but in 1868, she finally agreed to this and so *Victoria and Albert* (I)/*Osborne* (I) was broken up.

The next steam-powered royal yacht was also a nautical pioneer; the 317-ton *Fairy* was one of the first ships in the Royal Navy to have screw-propeller propulsion. The *Fairy* was also constructed of iron and was very fast for its time, being surprisingly successful against steam yachts built of wood or with partial wood hulls. It was designed and built by Thomas Ditchburn (1801–70); the keel was laid in 1844, at his company's shipbuilding yard, Ditchburn & Mare, Orchard Shipyard, Blackwall. The *Fairy* was also the first smaller royal yacht designed for use in harbour and river areas, where deeper-draught vessels were not able to go. Its dimensions were: a length between perpendiculars of 146 feet and an extreme length of 161 feet, a beam (extreme breadth) of 21 feet, and a mean draught of 7 feet. Its geared engines, with two oscillating cylinders, 42 inches in diameter by 36 inches in stroke, provided 128 (nominal) horsepower and were built by John Penn & Sons, Greenwich. The crankshaft rotated at 48 revolutions per minute and carried a spur-wheel of 9.7 feet diameter, which drove a pinion on the propeller shaft at the incredible speed of 240 rpm. Steam was supplied at 10 lb per

Figurehead of the Royal Yacht *Fairy*. (Colin White, Portsmouth Royal Naval Museum)

square inch in boiler pressure. The screw propeller was 5.3 feet in diameter with 8 feet pitch and was 1 foot long. The ship's speed was 12-14 knots, with an average of 13.25 knots. Coal stowage was 18 tons. The slender hull of *Fairy* was painted black, the main superstructure upperworks white and the single stove-pipe funnel yellow. It was rigged as a three-masted schooner.

The figurehead was of a young woman with no close resemblance to a fairy, armless, in a dress with a white bodice and green skirt and sleeves, with long blonde hair trailing to her shoulders. She is almost a replica of the figurehead on the royal yacht *Elfin*, except that version has black hair and a different treatment of the 'seeing' eyes by the craftsman who painted her. The origin of the name is not known, as 'fairy-like' was more applicable to the *Elfin* rather than the *Fairy*, the latter being a third larger than the former. The *Fairy* was launched in 1845, and commissioned at Portsmouth on 9 July that year. This was the year when the paddle-wheel versus the screw propeller contest took place, the *Alectro* against the *Rattler*, to decide future naval policy on ship propulsion.

Various trials and tests of endurance were held between the two ships. The *Rattler* won and paddle-wheel propulsion was phased out. Prior to this event, Francis Pettit-Smith, born in Hythe, Kent, a farmer on nearby Romney Marsh, was interested in ship propulsion and in 1835 invented a propeller activated by a spring that drove a ship model on a pond. In 1836, he built a boat and propelled it with an improved version. Encouraged by this, a full-sized ship of 237 tons, *Archimedes*, was built and tested his screw propeller at Sheerness. The Lords of the Admiralty were impressed and gave him an order for the propeller to be used in HMS *Rattler*, built at Sheerness, making it the first screw-propelled ship in the Royal Navy.

Although the *Fairy* had been considered only as a 'speciality' vessel because of its turn of speed at sea, which caused witnesses to comment that 'she was like a nautical greyhound', there was one occasion it was slower against a sister vessel, the *Wonder*, built in 1844 at Thomas Ditchburn's shipyard. In a race all along the South Coast of England to Southampton in 1845, the reason for which is unknown, unless it was to test *Fairy*, the *Wonder* arrived first at a speed of 14 knots, *Fairy* arriving later at a speed of 11 knots.

However, *Fairy*, with its shallow draught, successfully completed the duties for which it was built. One was to convey Queen Victoria on the Thames between Whitehall and Woolwich, and elsewhere along the river as required, in addition to its royal duties from Portsmouth to the Isle of Wight.

On 22 April 1854, Queen Victoria embarked on *Fairy* at Greenwich to be taken downriver to Blackwall in a procession of ships and other vessels to visit the *Great Eastern*, Isambard Kingdom Brunel's Atlantic cable-laying steamship. Presumably the Queen had decided to endure, as it was only a short distance, the noisome smells that arose from the contents of the river, which had caused several previously planned downriver trips on other occasions to be abandoned.

First, at the head of the procession, was the barge of the Lord Mayor of London, exercising his right to do so as the Conservator of the River Thames. Several river steamers and other vessels filled with passengers were astern of the royal yacht, some of them dressed in honour of the occasion, as were various small craft waiting at Blackwall to greet Her Majesty on arrival. Isambard Kingdom Brunel showed the Queen over *Great Eastern*, including the engines, and told her how they drove the paddle wheels and the screw propellers that would propel the huge ship. She was also shown models of the propellers and the now Sir Francis Pettit-Smith gave the Queen a gold model of the screw propeller used on the *Fairy*.

The *Fairy*, as the steam tender for *Victoria and Albert* (I), ferried the Queen, Royal Family, their visitors and the Queen's personal guests from Portsmouth to the Trinity House Quay, East Cowes, when she was living at Osborne House and spent much of the summer there. *Fairy* proved so seaworthy that it also served on sea cruises and in June 1845 had accompanied *Victoria and Albert* (I) to a naval event at Spithead and later that year taken the Queen and Royal Family on a cruise of the River Rhine, Germany. In 1846, the Queen, on a visit to Devon and Cornwall, even sailed in *Fairy* up the River Tamar. The *Fairy* also squeezed through the locks on the Caledonian Canal in 1847, when the Queen was visiting Scotland. On 17 July 1867, it took part in the vast Naval Review at Spithead with other royal yachts, including *Victoria and Albert* (II), *Alberta*, *Elfin*, and *Osborne* (II). When *Fairy* was replaced by *Elfin* and *Alberta*, it was taken over by the Admiralty and used for testing various types of screw propellers, in particular being fitted with a variable-pitch screw propeller. In January 1868, *Fairy* was stripped and taken to pieces. Her figurehead was preserved and is now in the Royal Naval Museum, Portsmouth. There is a model of *Fairy* in the Science Museum, South Kensington, London.

The second of several small royal yachts built to be used on shallower water and yet able to act as a tender to larger vessels was the 98-ton *Elfin*, a single-funnelled, two-masted, wooden-hulled, paddle-wheeled steam yacht, laid down at Chatham Dockyard in 1848. Designed and built by Mr Oliver Lang, its dimensions were: length between perpendiculars of 103 feet and an extreme length of 112 feet 3 inches, a beam of 13 feet 2 inches, and a draught of 4 feet 10 inches. Its oscillating engines, made by H. & G. Rennie of Blackfriars, provided 40 (nominal) indicated horsepower. Speed was 12 knots and coal stowage 7 tons.

Elfin's figurehead was almost a copy of the figurehead on *Fairy* – a young woman half-length, armless, and wearing an identical dress, with a white bodice and green skirt and sleeves. Upon *Elfin*, however, she is a black-haired beauty, her hair locks trailing to her shoulders and the 'seeing' eyes are open wider. Even so, both figureheads are so close in form they could have been carved by the same craftsman at the same time. The *Elfin* figurehead is also preserved in the Royal Navy Museum, Portsmouth. The origin of the name is uncertain; 'elfin' meaning, among other things, 'diminutive', 'small', is certainly true in comparison with other royal yacht tenders. *Elfin* was launched at Chatham on 8 February 1849, and commissioned at Portsmouth on 1 May that year.

The main and regular daily duty of the *Elfin* for some fifty-two years was to transport the royal mail, government correspondence and documents, the London newspapers and other materials, plus the Queen's Messengers, to and from Portsmouth to Cowes and Southampton. On 19 March 1901, it was paid off to be broken up the same year, although certain items were saved and retained at Portsmouth. Rather belatedly, on February 1929, the mainmast of *Elfin* was sent to Craigwell House, Bognor, to be used as a flag staff for the Royal Standard while King George V was living there for health reasons.

The replacement for *Victoria and Albert* (I) was the sleek and graceful *Victoria and Albert* (II). The keel of this three-masted, wooden-hulled, paddle-wheeled, 2,470-ton steamer with two bell-top funnels was laid down at Pembroke Dockyard on 6 February 1854. It was also designed and built by Oliver Lang. Its dimensions were: length between perpendiculars of 300 feet, a beam (breadth of hull deck) of 40 feet 3 inches, and a draught of 16 feet 3 inches. Its two-cylinder, oscillating steam engines, built by John Penn & Sons, Blackheath, provided 2,400 indicated horsepower. The engines made 21 revolutions per minute and were supplied by four boilers with six furnaces to each boiler. Coal stowage capacity was 350 tons,

Figurehead of the Royal Yacht *Elfin*. (Colin White, Portsmouth Royal Naval Museum)

the ship taking approximately 6 tons of coal to get up steam and approximately 3 tons an hour to maintain a maximum speed of 14.75 knots. The *Victoria and Albert* (II) was kept in such a state of readiness that only twelve hours' notice was required to prepare for the arrival of royalty and to get under way.

The hull, with its numerous white painted square ports, was black with a gold line and scrollwork on the bows and stern. The figurehead on the bows was, in fact, a Crowned Royal Coat of Arms, with a standard coloured centrepiece, the surround being gold painted on a white background. The funnels were primrose yellow ochre and the masts were brown varnished. The cabins on the upper deck and the ship's main superstructure and top part of the paddle boxes were white with beading that was gold lined. The davit boats, davits and anchors were black. At the date of the laying down of the keel, the ship's name had not been decided for certain and, for a short time, it was temporarily known as *Windsor Castle*. Because of the demands of the Crimean War, the ship's construction was delayed due to the diversion of materials and labour to the completion of several vessels needed for duty in the war zone in the Baltic. However, in less than a year from being laid down, the *Victoria and Albert* (II) received its name at a launching ceremony performed by Lady Milford on 16 January 1855. Furthermore, in the same month, in order to avoid confusion with the first *Victoria and Albert*, which was to remain in secondary service for another four years, the latter vessel was renamed *Osborne*, after Osborne House, the royal residence on the Isle of Wight. Towed by the tug *Dragon*, the jury-rigged *Victoria and Albert* (II) left Pembroke on 27 January 1855, reaching Portsmouth two days later. It was commissioned on 3 March and in April its machinery was installed and it completed its final sea trials in July 1855.

In 1894, a writer for *The Strand Magazine*, Mrs M. Griffith, was granted special permission by Queen Victoria to visit the new royal yacht and write about the experience and what she saw in detail for the magazine. Being an eyewitness of the ship's interior, I thought it of interest to include the actual words in her article entitled 'The Queen's Yacht':

What will first strike any visitor going on board the *Victoria and Albert* is the utter lack of luxury and magnificence of decoration and furniture in the Royal apartments. The most perfect simplicity, combined with good taste, prevails everywhere. It would be well for those who complain of the cost of our royal yachts to compare them with those of other nations and note the difference.

Criticism of expenditure by, presumably, Members of Parliament and others was not new in the respect of the royal yachts in earlier times. In other words, they were making the same comments in the nineteenth century as in the twentieth century regarding the *Britannia*, its operation and a possible replacement.

Mrs Griffith continued:

The deck is covered with linoleum, over which red carpeting is laid when the Queen is on board; and plenty of loungers and cushions laid about and many plants which contrast pleasantly with the white and gold with which the vessel is painted. She is lit electrically throughout, having forty-two accumulating cells. She carries two brass guns (six pounders) for signalling only. There is a pretty little five o'clock tea cabin on deck which has a hood coming down from the doorway as a protection from the wind. There is also a miniature armoury, lamp room, chart room and a number of lockers for signalling flags. All the Royal apartments have the floors covered with red and black Brussels carpet, in a

Figurehead Royal Coat of Arms on the Royal Yacht *Victoria and Albert* (II). (Colin White, Portsmouth Royal Naval Museum)

small coral pattern, the walls hung with rosebud chintz, box pleated, the doors of bird's eye maple, with handles of iron and fittings heavily electroplated. Her Majesty's bedroom has a brass bedstead screwed into sockets in the floor, bed hangings of rosebud chintz lined with green silk, canopy to match, green silk blinds and plain white muslin curtains with goffered frills, mahogany furniture, chintz-covered. There was also a towel horse with white muslin covers and bedsteps covered in green velvet. Dressing room: mahogany furniture covered with green leather, writing and dressing table combined; the walls covered with maps and charts on spring rollers. The Wardrobe Room, in which Her Majesty's dresser sleeps, is furnished in a similar style; and here I saw a boat cloak of blue embossed velvet, lined with scarlet, cloth, and another made entirely of scarlet cloth and with the 'Star' on the front which once belonged to George IV but is now sometimes worn by the Queen. In the Princess Royal's room, as it is still called, the furniture is of maple, an electric light pendant hangs over the toilet table, the walls are a pale salmon colour and the cornice a shell pattern in white and gold, the ceiling done in imitation plaster. The cabin which was formerly occupied by the Prince of Wales and Duke of Edinburgh contains two little brass bedsteads, maple furniture decorated with the Prince of Wales feathers; and the Tutor's cabin opens out of it. The Pavilion or Breakfast Room has mahogany furniture covered in leather and a couple of large saddle-bag easy chairs, a very handsome painted porcelain stove and frilled muslin curtains to all the ports. The Dining Room is furnished in a similar way but the salmon walls are hung with charts and portraits of the former captains of the vessel, who were as follows: 1. Lord Adolphus FitzClarence, 2. Sir Joseph Denman, 3. George H. Seymour, CB, 4. His Serene Highness Prince of Leiningen, 5. Captain H. Campbell and 6. Captain Frank Thompson. A very handsome candelabrum is of nautical design and the brass coal scuttle is fashioned like a nautical shell; walls, salmon; and cornice white and gold, in 'Rose, Shamrock and Thistle' design. Her Majesty's Drawing Room is 26 ft by 18 ft 6 ins. The walls chintz covered and hung with portraits of the Royal Family in oval gilt frames in the same design as the cornice; the furniture of bird's-eye maple; the coverings all of chintz to match the walls. Two large sofas, one at each end of the room, two or three easy chairs, the others high-backed; an 'Erard' piano, book case and cabinet combined, writing table, occasional tables, and an oval centre table comprise the whole of the furniture. I noticed a very handsome reading lamp of copper and brass, for electric light, with a portable connection, so that it can be used in any part of the room. The bells have also the same contrivance. The two chandeliers, for six candles each, are of the same design as the one in the Dining Room. The corridor leading to the Royal apartments is hung with rich green silk damask curtains and on the walls are watercolour paintings of several of Her Majesty's ships, done by the boys of Christ's Hospital. The staircase is very wide and handsome, of maple with gold and white balustrades. The Ladies-in-waiting have their cabins on the starboard side in the forepart of the ship and Lords-in-waiting on the port side, connected by corridors on each side to the Royal Apartments. They have also a commodious dining room in the forepart of the ship, also decorated in white and gold. Her Majesty's servants have twelve cabins, six of them fitted up for two people. In addition to these there are numerous domestic use offices, a dispensary, officers' cabins and accommodation for the crew which numbers 170. Her Majesty is never now staying on board more than forty-eight hours at a time but the vessel is kept in such perfect order that only twelve hours notice is required to prepare her for the reception of Royalty.

There ended Mrs Griffith's article and in the main she used facts, but some of her statements can be expanded. The forty-two accumulating cells to provide electricity were installed in 1888 to replace the original candle-power lighting although the Queen's silver candlesticks remained in her cabins 'just in case'. This installation was done only with the greatest reluctance on the part of the Queen, who insisted the royal yacht was to remain as the Prince Consort had planned it. However, on the advice of her oculist she finally gave permission for electricity to be installed. The linoleum on the upper deck was covered with red and black 'granite'-patterned carpet when the Queen was on board, but the floors of all the royal apartments were covered with red and black Brussels carpet in a small 'coral' pattern. The walls, as Mrs Griffith noted, were hung with a rosebud chintz, box pleated. The doors were made of bird's-eye maple with electro-plated fittings, but with ivory handles, not iron as Mrs Griffith had suggested. There were, in fact, two tea 'houses' or cabins on the upper deck, one being the 'pretty little five o'clock tea cabin'.

A feature not mentioned was the wing passages that ran under the shafts of the paddle wheels on the port and starboard sides of the Main or State Deck, to connect the quarters for the suite and the officers forward, with the Royal Apartments situated aft, which were entered by using double swing doors. Cabins on the port side, from forward to aft, were: the drawing room, the cabins of the Prince of Wales and his tutor, the valet's cabin, the bathroom and the royal pantry. On the starboard side from forward to aft ran: the Queen's wardrobe room, the Queen's bedroom, the Queen's drawing room (formerly the Prince Consort's dressing room), and cabins for the Princess Royal, her governess and dresser. Right aft was the breakfast room with square stern and side ports. There was a wide corridor between the State cabins and apartments that communicated with the upper deck by a staircase leading to the dining room lobby.

When considering the details of the Royal and State apartments, it must be remembered that the Prince Consort either designed the wall coverings and furniture, and planned the colour schemes, or had the over-riding say in what was installed. He, perhaps because of his German nationality, had an intense dislike of the garish, sometimes hideous and vulgar designs of furnishings and furniture of the day. His theme for *Victoria and Albert* (II) was not one of ostentation, but of simplicity with comfort.

The intention of the boat cloak, referred to by Mrs Griffith in 1894, was to be worn by the Queen in an open boat should the occasion arise to do so. It was still hanging in the Queen's wardrobe in 1904 when the *Victoria and Albert* (II) was broken up. The other example of clothing, 'scarlet cloth with a "Star" on the front that formerly belonged to George IV', was sometimes worn by the Queen in spite of it being his Order of the Garter.

Queen Victoria and other members of the Royal Family made their first cruise in *Victoria and Albert* (II) on 12 July 1855. It was a short trip around the Isle of Wight. Following this, with no royalty on board, it voyaged to the Scilly Isles to test it at sea under steam and sail power. It passed the trial superbly in a gale-force wind and a high sea running. Later that year, *Victoria and Albert* (II) conveyed Queen Victoria and Prince Albert to Boulogne on the occasion of a state visit to France to meet Emperor Louis Napoleon III. This was the beginning of a very busy career of almost fifty years in which this royal yacht carried both British and foreign royalty to and from Britain and took part in naval reviews and other functions.

On 23 April 1856, there was in a review at Spithead of the British Naval Fleet of some 250 warships. Eight royal yachts, with their tenders, were also present. In addition to Queen Victoria and Prince Albert, an illustrious assemblage of notables embarked at the Royal Clarence Yard, Gosport, on the *Victoria and Albert* (II) for this nautical event. These included Edward, Prince of Wales, the Princess Royal, Princess Alice, Princess Helena, the Duke of Cambridge, Prince Edward of Saxe-Weimar, and also the Lord Commissioners of the Admiralty, including Admiral Sir Edward Lyons, Commander-in-Chief of the Black Sea Fleet, Admiral Sir William Parker, Principal Naval ADC, Captain the Marquess of Townshend ADC, and the French Admiral Jurien de la Gravière. The concourse of warships, commanded by Vice-Admiral Sir George Seymour, flying his flag in an earlier royal yacht, *Royal George*, was anchored in two columns. One after the other these ships weighed anchor and passed before *Victoria and Albert* (II). When this manoeuvre had been completed, for the further entertainment of the party on the royal yacht, a signal was fired and a mock raid against the Spit Forts in the Solent was staged.

In 1857, several voyages were made by *Victoria and Albert* (II). The first was to take Prince Albert to Antwerp, Belgium, followed by a trip with him and Queen Victoria to Cherbourg and then to Alderney in the Channel Islands. Towards the end of the year, without royalty aboard, the ship went to Le Havre, France.

On 2 February 1858, *Victoria and Albert* (II) was chosen to convey the Princess Royal, eldest daughter of Queen Victoria and Prince Albert, from the Thames to Antwerp after her marriage to Crown Prince Frederick William of Prussia. In spite of the fact that it was snowing heavily, a large crowd had gathered to see the royal couple depart. During the voyage, the royal yacht had a collision with a brig and sustained minor damage to one of its paddle-wheel boxes.

Later in 1858, *Victoria and Albert* (II) went on a trial voyage to Ferrol and Corunna, Spain, without royalty on board; then to Portland with Prince Albert; then to Cherbourg with the Queen and her Consort; and finally, with them both aboard, set off from Gravesend to Antwerp. In 1859, this royal yacht was used by Princess Frederick of Prussia to visit Antwerp, by Prince Albert to go to the naval base at Portland, and by the Queen and Prince Albert to visit the Channel Islands. This routine continued in 1860. It sailed to Plymouth with Prince Albert and Edward, Prince of Wales, then to Antwerp with Queen Victoria and Prince Albert, and in November the Queen loaned *Victoria and Albert* (II) and *Osborne* to the Empress of Austria to take her and her companion, Princess Windischgrätz, from Plymouth to Madeira.

They left Plymouth at dawn on 24 November in calm weather but at about three in the afternoon a violent gale sprang up and lasted for three days, giving the ships, passengers and crew a rough voyage. On arrival at Madeira one of the Empress's servants wrote to her family:

> On Sunday the storm arose with such violence even some of the officers and crew were ill; from this moment no imagination can picture how terrible it was, the ship groaned and cracked in her innermost parts, she rose and tossed about and struggled with the foaming and furious waves, but when we reached the insidious Bay of Biscay it seemed as if all the evil water sprites had combined with the elements to destroy us ... During this time the second ship *Osborne* was sometimes seen tossing on the top of a terrible high wave, then the next moment nothing of her was visible but the extreme point of her mast so deep was she buried in the foam of the raging waves ... The night as it advanced was still more terrible, the storm increased more and its raging elements struck our ship as if it would have us for its prey ... In the intervals was heard the shrill sound of the boatswain's whistle, the increasing signals of the commander, the running and cries of the sailors, then a frightful crash which now I thought is the moment

when we shall all be buried in the deep sea ... Suddenly I was thrown from my bed which quickly followed me, but by great fortune it was stopped by a firm well secured table or else my leg and arm must have been broken. Everything about the Empress was scattered, looking-glass, china broken, chairs, tables, nothing escaped in Her Majesty's cabin nor in ours. The most useful necessary utensils were broken into a thousand pieces, in the kitchen all was ruin, the whole service of the Queen, glasses, pitchers, all was clatter and confusion ... Tuesday and Wednesday 27th and 28th we were blessed with brilliant sunshine, mild soft air; still, the motion was so strong we were forced to lie on the deck. At 7 o'clock on Thursday we anchored off Madeira and never in my life shall I forget with what feelings of gratitude and thankfulness I saw the noble rocky island rising before our eyes ...

Perhaps this description of part of the voyage was coloured by the thoughts of a person not accustomed to sailing in stormy weather on an open sea. Nevertheless, considerable damage had been done to the ship. Crew members sustained broken and dislocated limbs, bad sprains and cuts caused by falling from masts, down stairs or by being thrown about. The royal yacht was damaged. It sustained a rent in one side near to the stairs leading to the paddle wheels. But this damage did not delay it returning to England shortly after arriving at Madeira and disembarking its royal passengers.

In the spring of 1861, *Victoria and Albert* (II) again sailed to Madeira to embark the Empress and Princess for a cruise to Gibraltar and through the Straits of Gibraltar into the Mediterranean and on to Trieste from where they returned to Austria overland. This was the only occasion that *Victoria and Albert* (II) visited the Mediterranean.

Following this, there were voyages to Flushing, returning to Gravesend with the Crown Prince and Princess of Prussia, then to Portland with Prince Albert, and finally to and from Holyhead to Dublin with Queen Victoria and Prince Albert aboard. The death of Prince Albert on 14 December 1861 was to have a profound effect on the use of this royal yacht by the Queen. It caused her virtual withdrawal from public life for a number of years. Four lengthy voyages were made by other members of the Royal Family, but Queen Victoria used the ship sparingly and only for short voyages, just three in five years.

A happier occasion was in March 1863, when *Victoria and Albert* (II), escorted by HMS *Revenge* and HMS *Warrior*, sailed to Antwerp to bring Princess Alexandra of Denmark to England for her marriage to Edward, Prince of Wales, who had arranged for the cabin she was to use to be filled with roses. On 6 March, the royal yacht with its escorting vessels, arrived at The Nore and anchored off Margate for the night. The Mayor and Corporation of the Kent resort, accompanied by numerous high-ranking officers of the British Fleet, went aboard with an Address of Welcome for the Princess. Sheerness was illuminated and letters of blue lights ten feet high formed the word WELCOME along the seafront. Southend was also lit up and bonfires blazed on the shore on both sides of the Thames Estuary. On seeing these and numerous other forms of esteem for her, this then-little-known Danish princess was said, by her mother, to have been overwhelmed and asked: 'Are all these things for me?' The next morning the ships reached Gravesend where there were more scenes of tumultuous welcome as the Prince of Wales went aboard to greet his bride-to-be. On 10 March, the marriage ceremony took place and the same day *Fairy* took the royal couple from Southampton to the Isle of Wight and Osborne House. The only other voyage that year by the *Victoria and Albert* (II) was, yet again, to Antwerp, this time with Queen Victoria.

Early in 1864, Prince and Princess Louis of Hesse, who were regular visitors to England, were embarked at Flushing and conveyed to Gravesend. Edward, Prince of Wales, then used *Victoria and Albert* (II) for a voyage to Torbay, Devon, and then the ship returned Prince and Princess Louis of Hesse to Flushing. In 1865, the yacht made three voyages of note: taking the Prince of Wales to Holyhead and Kingstown (Dun Laoghaire), Prince Arthur, Duke of Connaught, to Milford Haven, and Queen Victoria again to Antwerp. Similarly in 1866, one voyage with royal passengers was to Cherbourg to embark the Prince and Princess Christian of Schleswig-Holstein. In 1867, a voyage to Portland with the Duke of Connaught was followed by a voyage to Antwerp to embark Prince and Princess Louis of Hesse. By now the crew must have known the way to Antwerp with their eyes shut for then it were an important port for travellers to and from Europe as are Ostend, Calais and Boulogne today. The *Victoria and Albert* (II), with four other royal yachts, took part in the Spithead Naval Review on 17 July 1867. Aboard with Queen Victoria was her guests, His Imperial Highness the Viceroy of Egypt and His Imperial Majesty the Sultan of Turkey, Abdul Aziz. After receiving a royal salute, the yacht steamed through the assembled lines of seventy-four ships. On the quarterdeck, during the review, the Queen invested the Sultan with the Order of the Garter. In 1868, the *Victoria and Albert* (II) took Prince Edward and Princess Alexandra to Holyhead and Kingstown, cruised the Norwegian fjords with the Princess of Leiningen, took Queen Victoria to Cherbourg, sailed to Flushing for Prince and Princess Louis of Hesse, and then sailed twice more to Cherbourg with Queen Victoria.

Towards the end of 1868, the royal yacht was given an overhaul, which revealed that the midships section was rotten and the vessel in an unseaworthy condition. The restoration work cost £52,000 and no voyages could be undertaken while it was being done. The rebuild and refit were completed in 1870 and soon after the *Victoria and Albert* (II) took Prince Edward and Princess Alexandra to Copenhagen to visit her family, then on to Elsinore, Denmark, followed by a cruise of the Baltic.

In 1871, *Victoria and Albert* (II) embarked the Crown Prince and Princess Frederick of Germany at Antwerp and on its return conveyed Prince Edward from Holyhead to Kingstown, followed by voyages to Plymouth and then back to Antwerp to return the Crown Prince and Princess Frederick of Germany, and embark Prince and Princess Louis of Hesse, to England. Early in 1872, she took Prince and Princess Louis of Hesse back to Antwerp, followed by a voyage to Cherbourg with Queen Victoria, then to Portland with Prince Edward and to Copenhagen with Princess Alexandra. In 1873, one voyage was made to Holyhead and Plymouth with Prince Edward. In 1874, there were just two voyages, both to Antwerp, one with the Duke and Duchess of Edinburgh, the second with the Crown Prince and Princess Frederick of Germany. In 1875, the yacht was again little used, making only one voyage of note – to Antwerp again with Prince and Princess Louis of Hesse. In 1876, it went twice to Cherbourg with Queen Victoria, but the following year made no voyages at all.

In 1878, there was a tour of inspection of Heligoland, an island off the mouth of the River Elbe in the North Sea, which was then a British possession. On board was Queen Victoria's third son, Prince Arthur, Duke of Connaught. This duty completed, *Victoria and Albert* (II) proceeded to Hamburg so Prince Arthur could visit the Emperor of Germany and then returned to Antwerp to embark the Duke and Duchess of Hesse-Darmstadt. Early in 1879, *Victoria and Albert* (II) made two voyages to Flushing to embark the Grand Duke of Hesse and bring him to England, the second to return him to that port. In March that year, it was used on the occasion of another royal marriage, sailing to Flushing to embark Prince and Princess Frederick Charles of Prussia and their son, Prince Frederick Leopold, and their daughter, bride-to-be Princess Margaret, and bring them to the gaily decorated pier at Queenborough, where they were met by Prince Arthur, Duke of Connaught, who had arrived there on the royal train. On 13 March, the Princess and the Duke were married at Windsor and at the end of the celebrations *Victoria and Albert* (II) took the Prince and Princess of Prussia and their son back to Flushing. Later that year, it was to take Queen Victoria and her daughter, Princess Beatrice, to Cherbourg, from where they would travel to Italy. In 1880, the yacht was little used, only taking Queen Victoria to Cherbourg and Flushing on a private visit and then taking Princess Louise, Marchioness of Lorne, to Liverpool.

When visiting European destinations, the Queen and other Royal Family members and their guests usually travelled by train to Gravesend – very occasionally to Queenborough – then by road from the railway station to a pier to embark on *Victoria and Albert* (II). The Prince of Wales also used the royal train to connect with the royal yacht, but he chose to leave for Europe from Port Victoria on the Isle of Grain and return there. The South-Eastern Railway had constructed a line to Gravesend and extended it in September 1882 across the flat expanse of the Isle of Grain – not really at that time an island – to a pier on the west bank of the River Medway, almost opposite the ports of Queenborough and Sheerness on the Isle of Sheppey. Patriotically, the railway company named it Port Victoria, the hope being that it would grow with its Port Victoria Hotel and pier into a thriving port in direct opposition to the London, Chatham & Dover Railway's pier at Queenborough. Unfortunately for them, this did not happen as a new dock and port facilities built at Tilbury on the River Thames were proving a more convenient and commercially viable option for ships sailing to and from Europe.

Later, however, the route from Gravesend to Port Victoria had its advantages for some members of the Royal Family. Due to its remoteness and sparse, scattered population, it was a quiet journey with only the shed-like stations of Sharnal Street, Stoke and High Halstow to pass through, so important travellers could relax, free of the crowds of onlookers that royal train journeys attracted. It was especially favoured by Edward and his companions en route to Europe. The port was used for passenger traffic until the First World War put an end to such voyages and the line and port were devoted to wartime activities. They reverted to peacetime use in 1919, but contact with the Royal Family and the royal yachts had disappeared due to changed circumstances. The line was closed in May 1951.

Several voyages of *Victoria and Albert* (II) in 1881 were short pleasure cruises for some of the other royals and their relations. One instance was a cruise in the English Channel visiting Lulworth Cove and Corfe Castle, presumably enjoyed by the Crown Prince and Princess of Germany with some of the British Royal Family. That same year, the Crown Prince and Princess were taken to Le Havre. The ship continued to be a 'royal taxi' in 1882, with several voyages to Flushing and Cherbourg with Prince Leopold, Queen Victoria and the Prince and Princess of Waldeck, a province in Prussia.

There were no voyages in 1883 and 1884 as *Victoria and Albert* (II) underwent another extensive refit. In 1885, it sailed to Flushing, Cherbourg and Antwerp with Queen Victoria and the Duke and Duchess of Connaught, later bringing the Grand Duke of Hesse and other guests from Flushing to England for the marriage of Princess Beatrice, the Queen's youngest daughter, to Prince Henry of Battenberg. During that time, 1883–85, Prince Louis of Battenberg, later First Marquess of Milford Haven, who was to play an important part in the fortunes of the Royal Navy, was serving as a Lieutenant on *Victoria and Albert* (II). He had hoped for a more active service appointment, having previously served in HMS *Agincourt* and HMS *Inconstant*, but his disappointment was tempered because when serving aboard the royal yacht he had more convenient opportunities to meet his fiancée, Princess Victoria of Hesse, whom he married in Darmstadt, Germany, on 30 April 1884.

In 1886, *Victoria and Albert* (II) conveyed Arthur, Duke of Connaught, to Plymouth and Carlos, the future King of Portugal, to Flushing, and took part in the celebration of the Colonial and Indian Exhibition with a Review of the Fleet at Spithead. For the next three years it continued work as a royal taxi, going twice to Cherbourg with Queen Victoria in 1887, and twice to Flushing. On the first voyage, the Queen was accompanied by the Crown Prince and Princess of Germany, on the second by the King of Saxony, who was also returning home. The ship also went once to Rotterdam with the Duchess of Albany and once to Plymouth and Lymington with the Crown Princess of Germany, after which it returned to Flushing with the Crown Princess of Germany and embarked the Duchess of Albany to bring her back to England. Also in 1887, there was another Review of the Fleet at Spithead, this time in honour of the Sultan of Turkey, with Queen Victoria and the Viceroy of India also on board. Queen Victoria went again to Cherbourg in 1888; the ship then sailed to Flushing and on to Cherbourg with her on board, then again to Flushing to embark Empress Frederick of Germany, and returning to Flushing with her early 1889. This year also saw two more visits with Queen Victoria to Cherbourg then to Antwerp to embark the Shah of Persia and his large retinue and later to return them to Cherbourg. In 1890, it sailed twice more to Cherbourg with Queen Victoria and to Flushing to embark the Empress Frederick of Germany, who was also on board later that year for a voyage to Gibraltar.

In 1891, *Victoria and Albert* (II) was again busy. It took Queen Victoria to Cherbourg, Empress Frederick of Germany to Flushing, and Prince Arthur, Duke of Connaught, to Pembroke and also to Portland, Tor Bay, Plymouth, the Scilly Isles and the Channel Islands. In 1892, Cherbourg and Flushing again saw the arrival of the royal yacht, firstly with Queen Victoria, then with the Prince and Princess Henry of Battenberg and Princess Christian of Schleswig-Holstein. Later that year, it again took the Duke of Connaught to Portland. The *Victoria and Albert* (II) continued to shuttle across the English Channel in 1893, going to Flushing for the Empress Frederick of Germany, to Cherbourg and to Flushing with Queen Victoria, to Flushing with His Imperial Highness the Tsarevich of Russia, to Portland with the Duke of Connaught, and to Milford Haven and the West Coast of Scotland with the Duke and Duchess of Albany.

The Empress Frederick of Germany went to Flushing en route for her home in 1894, Queen Victoria and Prince Louis of Battenberg were also conveyed to that port, and Prince and Princess Henry of Battenberg went to Guernsey. In 1895, *Victoria and Albert* (II) went to Cherbourg and Flushing with Queen Victoria and to Flushing with the Grand Duchess of Hesse, Prince and Princess Henry of Battenberg and King Carlos of Portugal. Queen Victoria went to Cherbourg in 1896 and the Duke and Duchess of Connaught went to Copenhagen, Kronstadt, and then up the River Neva to moor near the Nicholas Bridge, St Petersburg, on the occasion of the Tsar of Russia's Coronation. There followed a cruise in the Baltic and a visit to Stockholm. This was the last long-distance voyage *Victoria and Albert* (II) undertook. However, it continued to be of service to the Queen and was to have some final moments of glory.

In 1897, to commemorate Queen Victoria's Diamond Jubilee, a Naval Review was held at Spithead, where appraisals of the monarch's ships have been held since the fourteenth century, if not earlier. A vast concourse of British naval power was assembled there on 26 June. There were 165 ships, including twenty-one battleships, twelve first-class cruisers, twenty-seven second-class cruisers, numerous destroyers and other Royal Navy ships, stationed in four lines, each being five miles long. There was a fifth line of foreign warships representing their respective navies. On board *Victoria and Albert* (II) were the Prince and Princess of Wales and other members of the British Royal Family, together with Empress Frederick of Germany and representatives of all the European royal families and Heads of State of other nations.

During the year, *Victoria and Albert* (II) had conveyed Queen Victoria twice to Cherbourg. There is no doubt that these frequent, mostly short, voyages were a response to her loss of Prince Albert and a means of escape from the confinements of court and politics. However, due to her age and general withdrawal from public life, she spent only an average of forty-eight hours at a time on board. The ship had also fetched and returned Empress Frederick of Germany to Flushing and conveyed the Duke and Duchess of York to Holyhead and Kingstown, then to Belfast and a visit to the Clyde area. In 1898, another quiet year, Queen Victoria was taken to Cherbourg and the Empress Frederick of Germany was returned to Flushing. In 1899, on her one visit to France that year, Queen Victoria, now in her declining years, had been persuaded it would be more comfortable to travel from Folkestone in the SS *Calais-Douvre* to Cherbourg. To add to Her Majesty's comfort, some of the furniture was transferred from *Victoria and Albert* (II) to a specially built cabin for her on the *Calais-Douvre*. What the voyage was like has not been recorded, but the Queen apparently did not agree with the advice she had been given to travel in this way and on disembarking from the *Calais-Douvre*, although expressing satisfaction with the considerable amount of trouble that had been taking place, nevertheless said she would make the return journey in *Victoria and Albert* (II) – and that is what she did. On 6 May 1899, the *Victoria and Albert* (II), with the Duchess of York and Duke of Connaught aboard, visited Pembroke. Three days later the Duchess took part in the launching ceremony for the new royal yacht, *Victoria and Albert* (III), while *Victoria and Albert* (II) was present nearby. But the career of the latter was not quite at its close, although at the end of the Cowes Week racing season of 1899, knowing this was almost certain to be the last time it would be there with the Queen on board, the Royal Yacht Squadron had fired a twenty-one-gun salute as a mark of respect for this still gracious old ship.

However, in April 1900, Queen Victoria made her last voyage on *Victoria and Albert* (II), sailing from Holyhead to Kingstown on her visit to Ireland. She stayed at the Vice-Regal Lodge, Dublin, for three weeks and then returned to Holyhead. The *Victoria and Albert* (II) then went from Dartmouth and Plymouth to the Scilly Isles with Princess Henry of Battenberg and her children, followed by a cruise, in August, to Scotland's West Coast, carrying Princess Christian of Schleswig-Holstein and her two daughters.

In December 1900, the Queen was taken ill at Osborne House and died there on 2 January 1901. After her coffin had been conveyed by gun-carriage to Trinity Pier, East Cowes, on the afternoon of 1 February, seamen from the various royal yachts placed it on board the *Alberta* for conveying to Portsmouth. Preceding the *Alberta* were eight destroyers, the small royal yacht being followed by *Victoria and Albert* (II) acting as chief mourner, on board were the new king, Edward VII, his wife, now Queen Alexandra, the German Emperor Wilhelm II, Arthur, Duke of Connaught, other members of the Royal Family and members of the royal household. These ships were followed by the *Osborne* (II), the German Imperial

Yacht *Hohenzollern,* the Admiralty's *Enchantress* and Trinity House's *Irene.* From Cowes to Spithead the Channel and Reserve Squadrons of the Fleet were anchored in one line and minute-guns were fired by them as *Alberta* steamed past and by the ships in Portsmouth Harbour when she arrived.

This occasion almost marked the passing of *Victoria and Albert* (II) because its replacement was awaiting its duty. However, on the evening of 23 February 1901, King Edward VII, with two companions, boarded it at Port Victoria, Isle of Grain, and sailed early the following morning to Flushing. They then went overland to Berlin where the King's sister, Empress Frederick, was dangerously ill. On 2 March, *Victoria and Albert* (II) sailed from Flushing carrying King Edward VII to disembark him at Port Victoria, and then sailed to Portsmouth to be paid off on 3 December 1901, and passed into Dockyard Reserve at Portsmouth. There had been a slight hope the royal yacht might have one more role to play. Edward VII wanted it to be present at the Coronation Naval Review at Spithead in 1902. The proposal went so far as to ask Portsmouth Dockyard to survey the ship and to submit an estimate of the cost of refitting it for the Review, but this amount proved too high. So the proposal was very reluctantly abandoned. Despite his reluctance, Edward VII finally gave his permission for the ship to be broken up in 1904.

The *Victoria and Albert* (II) was towed by tugs to its end at the breakers' yard at Fareham Creek, Portsmouth. Some of the interior fittings were removed and passed on to *Victoria and Albert* (III). Certain items of furniture, the compass stand and binnacle stand were sent to Buckingham Palace. Two shelters went to HMS *Mercury* and the figurehead, quarter-badges, stern badges and steering wheels were sent to Portsmouth Naval Museum. Various items, including chairs, a desk and bookcase, the quarter-deck clock and some of the portraits of former captains, were transferred to the officers' quarters in *Victoria and Albert* (III). What remained of one of the most beautifully designed, comfortably accommodated and successfully operated royal yachts in the world was then burned.

The third royal yacht built to serve as a tender to *Victoria and Albert* (II) in succession to *Fairy* was *Alberta,* a two-funnelled, three-masted, paddle-wheeled, wood-hulled steam yacht. *Alberta* was laid down at Pembroke Dockyard in 1863. She was designed and built by the Admiralty Controller's Department, her dimensions being a length between perpendiculars of 160 feet, a beam of 22 feet 8 inches, a draught of 7 feet 9 inches, and a displacement of 370 tons. Her oscillating engines, made by John Penn & Sons, Blackheath, provided 1,000 indicated horsepower. She had a speed of 14 knots and coal stowage of 33 tons.

The *Alberta* was launched on 3 October 1863 and commissioned at Portsmouth on 30 November 1863. There are three possibilities for the source of the name. One: that the royal yacht was named after Victoria Elizabeth Mathilde Alberta Marie, Princess Victoria of Hesse, born in 1863, later Marchioness of Milford Haven. Two: that it was named after Princess Louise Caroline Alberta, Duchess of Argyll. Three: that it was named after Prince Albert, Queen Victoria's Consort, who had died in 1861. It is unlikely the ship was named after Alberta, the Canadian province.

Alberta largely took over the tasks formerly performed by *Fairy,* notably carrying the Queen and members of the Royal Family to and from Osborne House, Isle of Wight, and also on occasional pleasure sojourns at sea. A Naval Review was held at Spithead on 17 July 1867, attended by Queen Victoria on *Alberta* accompanied by the Sultan of Turkey and the Viceroy of Egypt. Dramatically, in 1875, with Queen Victoria, Prince Leopold and Princess Beatrice aboard, *Alberta* collided with the schooner *Mistletoe.* The Master and two passengers on *Mistletoe* were killed, but the royal personages were uninjured. It seems that *Alberta* took a diversionary course and *Mistletoe* did so too in the same direction and a collision was inevitable.

The *Alberta* was one of the royal yachts that performed a notable historic duty on 1 February 1901, by conveying the body of Queen Victoria on her last journey by sea from Trinity Pier, Isle of Wight, to a berth in the Clarence Yard, Gosport, from where the coffin was transferred to the royal train the next day.

After being paid off on 30 March 1912, in the reign of George V, *Alberta* was broken up in 1913. With its imminent withdrawal from service, plans were made for a replacement on the same lines, but smaller than *Victoria and Albert* (III). This was the *Alexandra*, named after Alexandra, daughter of King Christian IX of Denmark and wife of King Edward VII. This two-funnelled, three-masted, twin-screw propeller yacht of 2,050 tons was laid down at the A. & J. Inglis Shipyard, Glasgow, in March 1906. It was designed by Sir Philip Watts, Director of Naval Construction, and its dimensions were a length between perpendiculars of 275 feet, a beam of 40 feet, and a draught (extreme) of 13 feet. The two turbine engines were made by Parsons, the three boilers by Yarrow, providing 4,500 indicated horsepower. It had a speed of 18.86 knots and a coal stowage 250 tons.

The *Alexandra* was launched by Princess Louise, Duchess of Argyll, on 30 May 1907 and commissioned at Portsmouth on 7 May 1908. It was during 1908 that *Alexandra,* with *Victoria and Albert* (III), visited Tsar Nicholas II at Reval (now Tallin). It was also employed on various voyages across the English Channel and several other destinations of more sailing distance. In 1922, it took George V and Queen Mary from Dover to Calais on a State visit to the King and Queen of the Belgians who had been returned to Ostend in the *Alexandra* after a visit to England the previous year. As a royal yacht, *Alexandra* took part in Cowes Week and Naval Reviews, one of the latter being the Coronation Review at Spithead in June 1911. Not surprisingly, it was a great favourite of its royal namesake. At the outbreak of the First World War, its crew, with those of other royal yachts, were diverted to serve on Royal Navy warships.

The *Alexandra* was paid off at Portsmouth on 9 June 1922 and put up for sale. In 1925, it was bought by the Norwegian Shipping Company of Trondjheim, renamed *Prince Olaf* and used for pleasure cruising in the Norwegian fjords. In 1940, it was sunk during the German invasion of Norway.

The *Osborne* (II), named after the first *Osborne*, was much used by Edward and Alexandra when Prince and Princess of Wales for numerous pleasure cruises and semi-official visits, notably to the Mediterranean and countries such as Greece and Italy. Queen Victoria used it for crossing the English Channel and Edward, when Prince of Wales, did so for trips to Copenhagen with companions on his shooting party excursions. It was also brought into commission for official visits. This two-funnelled, three-masted, wooden-hulled, paddle-wheel steam yacht was laid down at Pembroke on 30 November 1868; the last paddle-wheeled royal yacht. Designed and built by E. J. Reed, its dimensions were an extreme length of 278 feet, a length between perpendiculars of 250 feet, a beam of 36 feet 2 inches, a breadth over paddle boxes of 62 feet 6 inches, a draught of 15 feet 1 inch, and a displacement of 1,850 tons. Its two oscillating engines built by Maudslay Sons & Field, Lambeth, provided 3,000 indicated horsepower and a speed of 15 knots. Coal stowage was 200 tons. The yacht was launched on 19 December 1870 and commissioned on 12 June 1874.

Osborne (II) was among the complement of ships accompanying the Prince of Wales in appropriate royal fashion on his Official Grand Tour of India in 1875. He embarked at Brindisi, Italy, on the suitably converted former Indian troopship

HM Yacht *Alexandra* being fitted out on the Clyde, Glasgow, 1908. (J & C McCutcheon Collection)

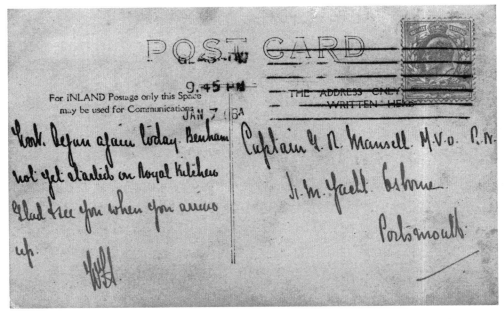

The rear of the postcard view above. Interestingly, it was sent to the captain of the *Osborne* (II). (J & C McCutcheon Collection)

Serapis, escorted by frigates HMS *Pallas* and HMS *Hercules* with *Osborne* (II) as attendant tender, en route to Malta, Piraeus, the Suez Canal, Bombay and Calcutta. It was a whim of the prince's, when on board a Royal Navy ship, to send the attendant royal yacht ahead while he entered a harbour last on board the RN ship. On this voyage, all went well until they reached Piraeus, the port for Athens, where Edward planned to meet the King of Greece. The Greek royal yacht *Amphitrite*, the entire Greek Navy and some of the Royal Navy's Mediterranean Fleet were assembled at the port to welcome him. Unfortunately, it then all went disastrously wrong. HMS *Serapis*, with Edward aboard, entered the harbour twice as fast as required. In an attempt to stop, the anchors were dropped, but the anchor cables parted. The engines full astern also failed to avert the consequent mishap. *Serapis* bumped into *Osborne* (II) and almost overwhelmed it, then collided with the Greek *Amphitrite*, smashing her bowsprit, and only avoided some of the other ships by the slightest of margins before coming to a halt just before hitting the harbour wall. Apart from the *Amphitrite* bowsprit, the damage was minimal and that was mainly to the Royal Navy's pride. More than likely Edward was amused by the scene, orders from embarrassed officers being flung loudly and the crew running in all directions to avoid chaos.

Afterwards, when sailing down the Suez Canal, Edward went aboard *Osborne* (II) to be put ashore to visit the Khedive of Egypt at Ismailia. Without further delays or disasters the ships arrived at Bombay on 8 November 1875. The purpose of the Grand Tour was fulfilled; the prince and his entourage toured India for four months, and re-embarked on *Serapis* at Bombay on 13 March 1876. On the decks of *Serapis* and *Osborne* (II) were housed animals and other livestock that had been gained on the Tour, some destined for the London Zoological Gardens. On the return voyage, the prince boarded *Osborne* (II) at Gibraltar to go ashore and visit King Alphonso XII of Spain and King Luiz I of Portugal. At Lisbon, he re-embarked on *Serapis* for the final part of the voyage to England, where he was met at The Needles Channel by his wife, Alexandra, awaiting him on the Admiralty yacht *Enchantress*.

Early in the career of *Osborne* (II), while sailing near Sicily in the Mediterranean late in the afternoon of 2 June 1877, Captain Pearson and two other officers saw through their telescopes 'a sea serpent' at a distance of 400 yards. Captain Pearson stated that he 'distinctly saw its seal-shaped head of immense size, large flippers and part of a huge body'. The two other witnessing officers were emphatic about what they saw. One said it had 'a head, two flippers and about thirty feet of an animal's shoulders. The head was about six feet thick, the neck narrower, about four to five feet; the shoulders about fifteen feet across, the flippers about fifteen feet in length.' The second witness said that it was 'a huge monster, having a head about fifteen to twenty feet in length; the head was round and full at the crown. The animal was swimming in a south-easterly direction, propelling itself by means of two large flippers or fins.' He said that he was also able to see part of the 'Monster's' body as it swam 'and that part certainly not under forty-five to fifty feet in length'.

A sad duty for *Osborne* (II), in 1884, was to sail to Cherbourg to bring back to England the body of Queen Victoria's fourth son, Leopold, whose death occurred in Cannes. For this duty the figurehead and gilt scrollwork of the royal yacht were covered with black cloth in mourning. *Osborne* (II) regularly attended Cowes Week with the Prince and Princess of Wales and other members of the Royal Family. It was also present at the Diamond Jubilee Review at Spithead in 1897. Among other final commitments, *Osborne* (II) performed a notable, but another sad, last duty. On Friday 1 February 1901, *Osborne* (II), following *Victoria and Albert* (II), accompanied the body of Queen Victoria on *Alberta* after its removal from Osborne House, to Trinity Pier, then to Gosport. *Osborne* (II) was also present as part of the through-the-ranks of ships by the royal yachts *Alberta, Victoria and Albert* (II), Kaiser Wilhelm's *Hohenzollern*, Her Late Majesty's battleships *Majestic* and *Prince George* and two destroyers. In 1908, *Osborne* (II) was sold and broken up at Felixstowe, Suffolk.

Because *Victoria and Albert* (II) had been a frequent floating home to her for some forty-five years, from the time when she was a young, married woman and her beloved Prince Albert, the Prince Consort, who had played a large part in the planning and designing of the interior, Queen Victoria resisted all attempts to replace it with a new royal yacht. Eventually, however, she could not forestall the inevitable and in January 1897 agreed to a new royal yacht being built, with the premise it must follow as closely as possible the exterior appearance and interior design of *Victoria and Albert* (II). Her love for this ship went as far as her insisting that the new one could not and would not be known as *Victoria and Albert* (III). She had no desire to share anything concerning 'her' Albert's royal yacht with a new ship he had had no part in, although it would be the Queen's royal yacht for future use in her service. 'The new royal yacht,' she said, 'was to be known as the *Balmoral*.'

Circumstances occurred and events unfolded in such a way that the Queen did not use the new royal yacht and never went on board it. In accordance with her wishes in respect of its predecessor, Sir William White, Director of Naval Construction, in August 1897, with Vice-Admiral Sir John Fullerton, Flag Officer Royal Yachts, discussed with Vice-Admiral Sir John Fisher, Controller, what features should be incorporated into the design. The Queen, as one example, had asked for more headroom at the top of a particular staircase to prevent her and others hitting their heads there. Sir William Whitehead and Sir John Fullerton went to Cowes and inspected *Victoria and Albert* (II) noting its interior fittings, furniture and accommodation. Shortly afterwards, Sir William Whitehead took a model of the new royal yacht, complete with the planned interior fittings and furniture to show Queen Victoria and other members of the Royal Family then present at Osborne House. The latter enthusiastically approved the proposals for the new ship and the Queen very reluctantly did so too. The principal features were to be a raised forecastle deck, a clipper stern and three funnels, later reduced to two. Having obtained Her Majesty's approval, the ship's keel was laid down at Pembroke Dockyard on 15 December 1897.

The *Victoria and Albert* (III) was a two-bell-top-funnelled, three-masted, twin-screw-propeller schooner yacht, steel-hulled and wood-sheathed – the reason for the wood cladding was to maintain an amenable level of temperature inside the ship. Designed by Sir William White, KCB, its dimensions were: an extreme length between perpendiculars of 380 feet, an overall length of 430 feet, a beam of 50 feet, a draught (extreme) of 20 feet 6 inches, and a displacement of 5,500 tons (deep draught). Its two vertical, four-cylinder inverted triple-expansion engines with eighteen Belleville water tube and coal-fired boilers provided 11,000 indicated horsepower, and were built by Humphreys, Tennant & Dykes Ltd, Deptford. Its maximum speed was 20 knots, with a range of 2,500 miles at 14 knots. Coal stowage was 714 tons.

In the same style as the *Victoria and Albert* (II), the hull, with its square, white-painted ports, was painted black. The ports were between two lines of carved, gold-leaf-gilded 'roping' ornamentation around the hull's sides. The figurehead on the clipper bows was a standard reproduction of the Royal Coat of Arms. The bowsprit above the figurehead was wood, brown varnished. The counter – the

The Royal Yacht *Osborne* (II) being broken up at Felixstowe, Suffolk, in 1908. (Taken by C. J. Emeny, Walton near Ipswich, and courtesy of S. Lilliman, Kempston, Bedforshire)

Osborne (II) being broken up at Felixstowe in October 1908. (J & C McCutcheon Collection)

Launching of the Royal Yacht *Victoria and Albert* (III), Pembroke Dock, on 9 May 1899. (Trindall & Co., Pembroke Dock. The photograph was given to the author by a former crew member, Lewis V. Tyler, Southsea, who in turn had been given it by an old dockyard worker who was present at the launching)

Victoria and Albert (III) when first commissioned; here seen with the raised forecastle that shortly afterwards had to be amended to correct the ship's stability. (Author's collection)

curved part of the stern of the ship – also had gilded scrollwork ornamentation. The funnels were buff-yellow, the masts were brown varnished and the colour scheme on the upper decks was white and gold leaf. When it was laid, there was a carpet on the upper deck with a red and black mixture pattern. If it came on to rain a pipe call was sounded and all hands off watch had to 'up carpets' as soon as possible. This task was avoided later by having special mackintosh covers that were laid quickly over the carpeting. The thirteen outboard davit boats, davits and anchors were black, and the boats were in black enamel.

The *Victoria and Albert* (III) was launched at Pembroke on 9 May 1899 by HRH The Duchess of York, later Queen Mary, accompanied by Arthur, Duke of Connaught and son of Queen Victoria. The ship was commissioned at Portsmouth on 23 July 1901. However, all did not go quite to plan. On 3 January 1900, a sensational incident had occurred involving the ship. During undocking by flooding from the dry dock at Pembroke, following the installation of machinery, boilers and masts, the ship had come off the blocks and slowly developed an alarming 25-degree list to port. To try to right it, water was pumped into the dock, then the ballast of 105 tons of pig iron paving dug up in the dockyard, and 200 tons of water was put in the bottom of the yacht. Eventually it was righted and floated onto an even keel, luckily the only damage being an eight-inch-deep, twenty-four-foot-long dent on either side of the yacht's double bottom.

The cause of this occurrence was simple. The ship was found by a Committee of Enquiry to have been top heavy with excess weight of 771 tons. About 400 tons were taken off the upper and main decks of the ship, in one form or another, to lighten the forecastle deck, funnels, masts and watertight doors, including a very heavy capstan on the forecastle. Having stabilised matters, the ship was thought seaworthy to leave Pembroke and reached Portsmouth safely. The incident was kept quiet for obvious reasons and the Queen was not told at the time. However, the London newspapers discovered the details and on learning what had occurred the Queen was not amused, in fact she was very angry. This debacle caused her to think the ship was 'unstable' and she vowed she would never sail anywhere on it, and she didn't. As far as is known, she only saw *Victoria and Albert* (III) once 'in person', when the ship was sailing through the Solent to Portsmouth and passed the Isle of Wight.

Several months after *Victoria and Albert* (III) was commissioned, it became evident that the ship was not as it should be, especially during rough weather, seeming to confirm the Queen's opinion. So it returned to Pembroke Dockyard to have various alterations done to improve its stability. The short forecastle was removed, the main and mizzenmasts were stepped further aft and more ballast added. However, even after these alterations, this royal yacht was not a 'comfortable' ship in a heavy seaway; in such conditions it had a corkscrew motion and a somewhat alarming roll. In 1908, on a voyage to the Baltic and a rendezvous with the Tsar of Russia, it was recorded that a number of those on board, including King Edward VII, Queen Alexandra and the First Sea Lord, Sir John Fisher, were seasick or otherwise decidedly unwell. In one alarming incident, Queen Alexandra, still sitting in her chair, was suddenly thrown from one side of the dining saloon to the other side, teapots, cups and saucers and other table items hurtling after her with a crash and breaking. Fortunately, Queen Alexandra was not hurt.

Captain Augustus Agar, VC, was Lt Commander on *Victoria and Albert* (III) during 1924 and 1925, and in his autobiography, *Footprints in the Sea*, he described the accommodation of the ship at that time:

Victoria and Albert (III). (J & C McCutcheon Collection)

Victoria and Albert (III) in Southampton Docks, 1933. (J & C McCutcheon Collection)

The internal construction and arrangements naturally centred around the royal apartments. They followed very closely those of her predecessor. The reception rooms and dining saloon were on upper deck level, while the cabins and other private suites and rooms were one deck below. Ample space, therefore, had to be allowed on the upper deck for receiving guests, making presentations and so on. For this purpose the upper deck from right aft as far as the bridge of the ship was fitted with carpets. These had to be taken up by sailors whenever it rained and included two strips, one for each side of the ship, 200 feet long and known by the men as the 'serpents'. Above the upper deck on a boat deck level four small sun parlours known as tea-houses took the place of the boats which would normally have been stowed inboard. These small parlours trapped all the sun available, and being sheltered from the wind with an all-round view, were very cosy indeed.

The wardroom and officers' cabins were under the bridge. These were most comfortably furnished and upholstered but following the Victorian tradition there were no bathrooms. I had my bath every morning in a small tin tub brought into my cabin by Watts, my Marine servant, with two cans of water and as far as I can remember everyone else did the same, including most of the royal suite.

The men's quarters were forward of the bridge. They were quite comfortable but rather cramped at sea because we took on a few extra staff when 'on service', plus the Royal Marine band, for which accommodation had to be found. At that time we were the only ship in the Navy allowed a 'wet' canteen, i.e. the men were allowed to have their own beer on board and, of course, never abused the privilege. There were about thirty Court servants of varying degree ranging from the Sergeant Butler to the lesser kitchen staff. Except for a few upper servants their quarters were very cramped, but they never complained and the discipline

The writing and business room on the Royal Yacht *Victoria and Albert* (III). (J & C McCutcheon Collection)

'From warship to yacht', the Princess of Wales' apartment. (J & C McCutcheon Collection)

they kept among themselves was truly fine. Never have I seen servants who knew so exactly what service was and took real pride in their job without presumption or reward.

There were fourteen cabins for guests, with a further seven for the maids and valets. In the stern the original Royal Household Dining Room was converted at the command of King Edward into three cabins; one for three servants, one for the Superintendent of Police and one as a Post Office. A smoking room, reception lobby and dining room were in a pavilion on the upper deck. A grand staircase led to the main or State deck and to the State corridor from which, proceeding forward on the starboard side, opened access to the Royal Quarters, including the King's Writing Room, the King's Dressing and Bathrooms, the King's Bedroom, the Queen's Bedroom, the Queen's Dressing and Bathrooms, the Queen's Dresser's cabin. Proceeding forward on the port side was the bedrooms for the Prince and Princesses, a dressing room, also the Dressers' and Valets' cabins. Some of the Royal Household had accommodation rear of the entry ports, the royal servants being on the deck below it. The ship's officers and crew had their basic accommodation forward of the funnels.

The first official task of *Victoria and Albert* (III) was the sad one, conveying Edward VII to Flushing en route to the funeral of his sister, Empress Frederick of Germany, in 1901. Following this, without royalty aboard, it sailed to Lisbon and Gibraltar for sea trials and passed them admirably. In March 1902, Edward VII and Queen Alexandra visited Dartmouth on the royal yacht to lay the foundation stone for the Royal Naval College. Then in May, with Prince Arthur, the Duke of Connaught aboard, it sailed to Bilbao, for the Duke to attend the Coronation of King Alphonso XIII at Madrid. In June, after his sudden illness, Edward VII went on a convalescence cruise around the Isle of Wight. On 16 August, carrying Edward and Alexandra, *Victoria and Albert* (III) took part in a Coronation Review, then,

Victoria and Albert (III) at Ballachulish. (J & C McCutcheon Collection)

Victoria and Albert (III).

Some of the Royal Family, guests, Royal Household staff and Ship's Officers on *Victoria and Albert* (III). The occasion was their return from Norway when King Haakon VII of Norway, married to Edward VII's daughter Princess Maud, was crowned on 22 June 1906. The central woman in white is Princess Mary, later Queen Mary, and on her left is Commodore Keppel. On her right, although a handwritten caption states it is Princess Victoria, the author thinks this is a slip and it is Queen Alexandra. The girl is Princess Mary. Behind her stands the Prince of Wales, later George V. The civilian on his left is Sir Francis Laking, the King's physician. The seated man far left in the white-peaked cap is Dr Fridtjof Nansen, the Norwegian polar explorer and first Norwegian ambassador to the United Kingdom. The photograph was taken by John J. Griffiths, a commercial photographer from Sheerness, while the ship was lying off the port. (Given to author by Edna Colyer, Gosport, daughter of John Griffiths)

with its royal passengers, called at Portland, Milford Haven, the Isle of Man and various ports along the West Coast of Scotland to disembark the King and Queen at Invergordon. It then docked at Queensferry to await Queen Alexandra and take her on her annual autumn cruise to Christiansund (Kristiansand) to visit her daughter, Maud, who had married her cousin, Prince Carl of Denmark, in 1896. He took the name Haakon when he was elected King of Norway in 1905. Queen Alexandra then voyaged on to Copenhagen.

In 1906, *Victoria and Albert* (III) conveyed members of the Royal Family, guests and members of the royal household to Norway for the Coronation of King Haakon VII at Trondheim on 22 June. Among those on board for the voyage were George, Prince of Wales, later George V, Princess Mary, later Queen Mary, another Princess Mary, Commodore Colin Keppel, Lady Trefussis, and Sir Francis Laking, King Edward's physician. The royal yacht returned to England on 5 July, anchoring off Sheerness, Isle of Sheppey. It was decided to have a photograph taken of those assembled on deck, perhaps because there were important extra guests on board, including polar explorer Dr Fridtjof Nansen, who, in 1905, was involved in negotiating the separation of Norway from Sweden and had become the first Norwegian Ambassador to the United Kingdom. For some unknown reason, there was not an official photographer on board so one of the royal household staff went ashore to find one. Photographs on display in the Sheerness premises of John J. Griffiths were found to be of the required high standard and he was commissioned to undertake the task. His daughter, Mrs Collyer, recalled in a letter to the author that her father was 'commanded' to take the photograph aboard the yacht. Orders were placed for copies, therefore, those depicted must have been pleased with the result. It was, however, the only photograph of a royal yacht group taken by John Griffiths, who kept a copy for his archive, too (see p. 68).

From 1901 until 1910, *Victoria and Albert* (III) was kept busy taking King Edward VII, Queen Alexandra and other members of the Royal Family on a large number of visits to Europe and Mediterranean countries for official functions or pleasure cruises. A few were as follows. In March 1903, it sailed to Lisbon, Portugal, with King Edward VII to meet King Don Carlos I of Portugal, who visited the ship on 2 April. After this King Edward sailed on to Gibraltar, Algiers, Malta, then Syracusa and Rome where he disembarked and came home overland. In 1904, the King visited Germany and Kaiser Wilhelm II, embarking at Port Victoria on 23 June and arriving at Brunsbüttel on 24 June and sailing into the Kiel Canal. The Kaiser, hoping to impress Edward, sent detachments of his crack cavalry, armed with lances topped with white pennants, to provide an escort for the royal yacht from the canal bank. Unfortunately, there were boggy areas on the bank and some of the horses unceremoniously dumped their riders into the mud. At Holtenau, Kaiser Wilhelm, the German Crown Prince and Prince Henry of Prussia boarded the royal yacht and at Kiel the assembled German Fleet fired a royal salute. Perhaps also to impress Edward, he was taken to inspect the

Royal Yacht *Victoria and Albert* (III), with King Edward VII on board, steaming along the Kiel Canal on 24 June 1904. The white dots, above right, are the white pennants on the lances of Kaiser Wilhelm's mounted cavalry that escorted the ship. (Given to author by Lewis V. Tyler, Southsea)

Germania and other shipyards and have lunch with Admiral von Koester on board the *Kaiser Wilhelm* (II). In August 1905, Edward VII attended a Review at Spithead of some of the British and French Fleets in connection with the Entente Cordiale between the two countries. In the spring of 1906, Edward and Alexandra, with the Countess of Antrim and Hon. Charlotte Knollys, embarked at Marseilles for a cruise to Sicily, then on to Corfu where they met the Queen's brother, the King of the Hellenes, aboard the Greek royal yacht *Amphitrite* in the harbour. The two ships then cruised along the Greek coast to Katakolo, the port for Olympia. *Victoria and Albert* (III) sailed on to Naples, where Edward disembarked to return overland to London. Queen Alexandra stayed aboard to cruise to Rome and visit Florence and Venice. She rejoined the royal yacht at Leghorn and went on to Malaga and Lisbon where she visited the King and Queen of Portugal, returning to Weymouth and Portsmouth six weeks after the start of the cruise. In the summer of 1906, *Victoria and Albert* (III) made the previously mentioned voyage to Norway for the Coronation of King Haakon VII. The ship was used for a visit to the Tsar of Russia at Reval in 1908, and to the opening of the new Royal Edward Dock at Avonmouth and for a visit to Copenhagen. However, for Edward this was all shortly to end. In the spring of 1910, Queen Alexandra took another cruise to the Mediterranean to visit her brother, the King of the Hellenes. She disembarked at Venice to return overland to London, arriving on 5 May. King Edward VII died on 6 May, while the royal yacht was still at sea on its way back to Britain.

The now-widowed Alexandra continued to use *Victoria and Albert* (III) as before. Accompanied by her daughter, Princess Victoria, she sailed from Dundee on 19 September 1910 to Copenhagen to meet family and friends. Early in 1911,

Victoria and Albert (III) in about 1911. Place and photographer are unknown. (Harold Parks, Sheerness)

Victoria and Albert (III) with the King aboard, inspecting the fleet.
(J & C McCutcheon Collection)

The Royal Yacht *Victoria and Albert* (III) at Weymouth, May 1912.

Royal Yacht *Victoria and Albert* (III) with HM King George on board watching the combined fleets proceed to sea at Spithead, 20 July 1914. (J & C McCutcheon Collection)

again with Princess Victoria, she went to Corfu to meet her brother, the King of the Hellenes, and also Kaiser Wilhelm II. That same year, and in 1912, she undertook her usual cruise to Kristiansand and Copenhagen, but in 1913, as the war clouds gathered, the voyage was direct to Copenhagen.

King George V, who loved sailing, but not by ship to places far away from the United Kingdom, used *Victoria and Albert* (III) on 26 July 1910 to review 135 Royal Navy ships in Tor Bay. In October, the yacht was despatched in haste to Gibraltar to collect the deposed King Manuel of Portugal, his family, Queen Amelie, and the Duke of Oporto. Manuel had escaped a rebellion against him by sailing on his yacht *Amelia* (III) to safety at Gibraltar.

On 24 June 1911, preceded by the Trinity House yacht *Irene* and followed by *Alexandra,* the Admiralty yacht *Enchantress* and the Commander-in-Chief's *Firequeen,* the *Victoria and Albert* (III) took part in the Coronation Review at Spithead. On board were King George and Queen Mary, Edward, Prince of Wales, Prince Albert George, Princess Mary together with nobility and government leaders who had attended the Coronation, plus representatives of the armed services. The assembled ships included 167 Royal Navy ships and eighteen foreign warships from other important maritime nations. Between 1901 and 1939, *Victoria and Albert* (III) attended three Coronation Reviews – in 1902 for Edward VII and Queen Alexandra, in 1911 for George V and Queen Mary, and in 1937 for George VI and Queen Elizabeth.

Following the Coronation Review, George V and Queen Mary voyaged to Ireland, then to Caernarvon to attend the investiture of their son, Edward, as Prince of Wales. In May 1912, George V went on it to visit the Fleet at Portland to see a display by the new flying machines – aeroplanes – and have a short underwater cruise in submarine D4. In June, George V and Queen Mary went by sea to Cardiff to lay the foundation stone of the Welsh National Museum.

The days of pleasure usage for this royal yacht came to an end in 1914. On 19 July, the King was aboard her to witness the huge mobilisation of the Home Fleet at Spithead and the next day she was the lead ship when the Fleet put to sea. In August 1914, both *Victoria and Albert* (III) and *Alexandra* were laid up for the duration of the war and put in the care of the Keeper and Steward of the Royal Apartments.

A fine body of men: the successful *Victoria and Albert* (III) football team, 1931–32. (Taken by Thomas Humphries, presumably in Portsmouth judging by the masts top right. Given to the author by Mrs Ethel Pook, Gosport, whose husband was Shipwright Officer on the ship.)

Victoria and Albert (III) in 1932. The three flags indicate royalty was on board; the ship being under way the Royal Coat of Arms in lieu of the figurehead is clearly visible. Event, time and photographer are unknown. (Given to author by Mrs Ethel Pook, Gosport, whose husband was Shipwright Officer on the ship for seven years.)

Members of the Royal Family and their guests, Royal Household staff, with Officers, on board *Victoria and Albert* (III), Cowes Week, 1933. Central are King George V and Queen Mary. On the King's right is the Duchess of York, later Queen Elizabeth. On Queen Mary's left is her son, the Duke of York, later George VI. (William Kirk & Son, Cowes. Given to author by Mrs Ethel Pook, whose husband was Shipwright Officer among the crew.)

The assembled complement of *Victoria and Albert* (III), Cowes, 1933. It was the tradition at the end of Cowes Week to have such a photograph taken on board the ship. The central figure in white is Queen Mary, on her left is her son, Duke of York, later George VI. On her right is her husband George V and on his right is the Duchess of York, later Queen Elizabeth. (Russell & Sons, Southsea. Given to the author by Mrs Ethel Pook, whose husband was Shipwright Officer on the ship.)

HRH Duke of Kent with his mother Queen Mary by an aft upper deck staircase on *Victoria and Albert* (III), Cowes Week, 1934. (William Kirk & Son, Cowes. Given to the author by Mrs Ethel Pook, Gosport, whose husband served as Shipwright Officer on the ship for seven years.)

King George V and Queen Mary on board *Victoria and Albert* (III). (J & C McCutcheon Collection)

Members of the Royal Family and their guests, Royal Household staff and Officers on *Victoria and Albert* (III), Cowes Week, 1934. Queen Mary in white is central, on her left is her husband George V and on her right is her son Duke of Kent. (William Kirk & Son, Cowes. Given to author by Mrs Ethel Pook, whose husband was Shipwright Officer on the ship.)

In 1919, *Victoria and Albert* (III) was re-commissioned and in 1920, with George V and Queen Mary aboard, visited West Country ports and the Clyde. The yacht was used three times in 1921 and twice in 1922, and only for regattas on the East Coast and Cowes Week in 1923. During George V's reign, it continued to be present at Cowes Week and at the Clyde Regattas in Scotland. George V was unwell with respiratory problems in late 1924, so it was suggested that he should take a cruise for his health's sake only, with no official duties, to which he reluctantly agreed. On 20 March 1925, *Victoria and Albert* (III), with King George and Queen Mary, and some of their friends and members of the royal household staff, sailed from Genoa to Leghorn, then to Pisa where they saw the Leaning Tower, but only Queen Mary went into its interior. The cruise of the Italian Coast continued, the yacht putting in to Naples, Messina, Syracusa, Taormina and Palermo, returning to Genoa on 23 April.

From 1925 to 1932, the royal yacht was only used by George V in Cowes Week for accommodation and occasional social purposes. On 11 July 1932, the King, with Prince Edward and Prince Albert George, left Portsmouth for Weymouth to view the gathered Fleet the same evening. On the following three days they watched a number of naval exercises, sailing exercises, and aircraft flying displays. On the final day, 14 July, the *Victoria and Albert* (III), as part of the Fleet, went to sea for those on board to watch more naval exercises, returning to Portsmouth in the evening. On the previous evening, the King had been a hospitable host aboard the royal yacht to the various Flag Officers and ships' Captains.

The last ceremonial occasion the *Victoria and Albert* (III) took part in with George V on board was the 1935 Silver Jubilee Naval Review. From 15 to 17 July,

The Royal Yacht *Victoria and Albert* (III) passing through the lines of the fleet with the King and Queen on board, as seen from the *Queen Elizabeth*. (J & C McCutcheon Collection)

Victoria and Albert (III).

at Spithead, there were exercises by the Fleet, including the First Battle Squadron of the Mediterranean Fleet, comprising of HMS *Queen Elizabeth*, HMS *Ramillies*, HMS *Revenue*, HMS *Resolution* and HMS *Royal Sovereign*. George V, Edward, Prince of Wales, Albert George, Duke of York, and George, Duke of Kent, used the royal yacht as accommodation while at Portsmouth. The royal train took them to Cosham, from where they travelled by car to Portsmouth Dockyard, the yacht being moored at the South Railway jetty. On being met by the Commander-in-Chief, Admiral Sir John Kelly, and the Admiral Superintendent, Vice-Admiral Sir Henry Kitson, a royal salute was fired by the Naval Saluting Battery. As the King and royal party went aboard, the Royal Standard was broken out at the mainmast. When the royal train had reached Cosham, the signal 'Dress Ship Overall' had also been given to the assembled warships from the Dockyard Signal Tower. The King and royal party slept aboard and on 16 July sailed through the lines of manned ships of the Fleet, and then led the Fleet to sea for the exercises. The Silver Jubilee Naval Review, which had begun with a rocket being fired from the royal yacht, ended with a firework display, followed by the brilliant lighting up of the outlines of the Fleet's capital and flagships funnels, hulls, masts, superstructure, flags and illuminated crowns with the letters GR.

As usual in August, *Victoria and Albert* (III) attended the 1935 Cowes Week, with George V and Queen Mary, and the Duke and Duchess of York (later George VI and Queen Elizabeth) aboard. They would sometimes travel by royal train to the South Railway jetty at Portsmouth and, on boarding, the ship's officers would be lined up on deck to receive them. Not surprisingly, Cowes Week was always a busy time for the crew as everything had to be perfect and ship-shape, but none would have wanted to miss the occasion. During its winter lay-up, *Victoria and Albert* (III) had two new masts and two booms fitted, made of timber from the forests of Vancouver Island, British Columbia, Canada.

In an article in the *Portsmouth Evening Herald* on 20 July 1936, headed 'Story of the *Victoria and Albert* – Floating Home of the Royal Family', Angela Fitzroy, at that time 'a well known writer on royalty', commented:

Victoria and Albert (III) with the Sovereign on board, foreground, reviewing the Fleet at Portland outside the breakwater. Ships are: left, HMS *Nelson* battleship; centre right, HMS *Rodney* battleship; right, HMS *Hood* battlecruiser. (A. Berry, Colchester)

Yachtsmen declare that Cowes would not be Cowes without the *V. and A.* With the attendant warship hard by the old yacht is the most familiar sight of Cowes during the famous regatta in the first week in August and she carries out her duties of housing the Royal Family with true dignity. While she is not a first class sea boat, as is widely known, nobody can deny her handsome appearance and the dignity with which she carries herself. One can understand that the Navy regards service in her as a high honour. There are about 350 Royal Navy men on board and they take extreme pride in her. She is always kept in commission so that she is ready for sea at practically a moment's notice. Her crew are a happy family and the ship is kept spotless from end to end. The decks are, as the saying goes, 'fit to eat off', and the engine room is burnished to a nearly dazzling brightness. King George was always proud of the engines of the *Victoria and Albert* and often visited them with guests he was entertaining.

But, although the *Victoria and Albert* is a possession of the Royal Family, there is nothing flashy about her. In every way she reflects the character of the Royal House, in that although comfortably furnished there is no ostentatious display. When first built Queen Victoria had her modelled on the earlier yachts of the same name and would have nothing altered but since then it has been essential to bring the ship up to date. King Edward (Edward VIII) who had visited the *V. and A.* while inspecting the Fleet off Portsmouth, is having many alterations effected.

After Edward VIII's visit on 30 June 1936 to see the results of this partial refit, the royal yacht undertook a short cruise, with no royals on board, and anchored in Weymouth Bay, off Falmouth and Torbay, and returned to Portsmouth. On 12 November, using *Victoria and Albert* (III) as accommodation, Edward VIII was at Portland to view some of the Fleet and afterwards held a dinner for officers aboard her.

Angela Fitzroy's article continues:

Only a few years back Queen Mary had the kitchens modernised and more comfortable quarters, including a tiled bathroom for the officers, installed. There

Royal Yacht *Victoria and Albert* (III)'s reception lobby. (J & C McCutcheon Collection)

The corridor on the Royal Yacht *Victoria and Albert* (III). (J & C McCutcheon Collection)

are cabins for various members of the Royal Family, but none of them is lavishly furnished. King George had a small sitting-room, with a settee and a few easy chairs and every year before he went to Cowes a selection of his favourite books was sent down for his holiday reading. Next door was the office of his private secretary, for even when away from London the duties of State necessitated him being kept in constant touch with the capital. Then there were his bedroom, a bedroom and a boudoir for Queen Mary and similar apartments for the Prince of Wales, as King Edward then was, and the Princess Royal. The walls of these apartments are tastefully draped with patterned cretonne, the ports being fitted with silk curtains.

On the upper deck is the saloon, where it has been the practise to hold intimate dinner parties, one of the outstanding features of Cowes Week. There their Majesties entertained many of their closest friends and all formality was abandoned. King George was a naval man to the end of his life and the special 'den' for himself and his friends in the naval and yachting worlds was the smoke room, which is fitted out in mahogany.

One of the most treasured relics in the yacht recalls one of the most heroic deeds in the history of Britain. This is a tattered White Ensign, which was brought back from the Antarctic by Admiral Evans. It was found still braving the Antarctic blizzards, flying over the little tent that held the bodies of Captain Scott and his noble companions.

There ended Angela Fitzroy's article, on a patriotic note.

A correspondent whose family had served on royal yachts, Mrs Beryl Powell, recalled for the author some pre-1939 personal visits to the *Victoria and Albert* (III):

> On three occasions I visited the royal yacht and had tea. My mother had a friend whose father was Keeper of the Royal Apartments and so we were invited by him and twice we took friends with us, one of whom took these snapshots. [See 82–83.]
>
> The cabins were all in different coloured chintz with the name above each door, i.e., Prince of Wales, Princess Mary, Prince George, etc. King George V's cabin was in royal blue and gold and Queen Mary's was, I think, in pale green and gold. The yacht was, of course, spotless. We usually went on board just after Cowes Week and I remember how very smart and polite the crew were.

It had been assumed that Edward VIII, after improvements were made to his requirements, would use *Victoria and Albert* (III) for a summer cruising holiday with Mrs Simpson in the Mediterranean. Instead, he chartered the 300-foot *Nahlin*, built by John Brown & Co., on the Clyde, for Lady Yule in 1930. Due to his abdication on 11 December 1936, Edward VIII had no further contact with *Victoria and Albert* (III). The *Nahlin*, like the abdicated king who pleasured on it, seems also to have had a restless career. In 1937, King Carol of Roumania bought it for £120,000 to please his mistress, Magda Lupescu, renaming it *Luceafarul*. However, when he too had to abdicate in 1940, the *Nahlin* became Roumanian state-owned and rather ignominiously, or perhaps aptly knowing Carol's former lifestyle, was used as a floating restaurant on the River Danube from 1980. It was bought by Nicholas Edmiston, a yacht broker, and surveyed for restoration at Devonport in 1999. (See Roumania Royal Yachts, page 139–40.)

Despite this unfortunate start, *Victoria and Albert* (III) continued to give many years of useful, reliable service. In May 1937, George VI, Queen Elizabeth, Princess

Overleaf and this page: Snapshots of various parts of *Victoria and Albert* (III), August 1924. (Mrs Beryl Powell, Havant)

The *Nahlin*. (J & C McCutcheon Collection)

HM King George VI escorted by torpedo motor boats at the opening of the Imperial Maritime Exhibition, 27 April 1937. (J & C McCutcheon Collection)

An informal photograph of HRH Princess Elizabeth with HRH Princess Margaret aboard *Victoria and Albert* (III) during a Cowes Week in the 1930s. (Taken by a deceased crew member and given to the author by his shipmate, also a former crew member, Lewis V. Tyler, Southsea. Published by gracious permission of Her Majesty The Queen.)

King George VI and Queen Elizabeth, with Princess Elizabeth and Princess Margaret aboard the *Victoria and Albert* (III) in 1937. Place and occasion is unknown, possibly Cowes Week or Portsmouth. (Russell and Sons, Southsea. Given to the author by Mrs Ethel Pook, Gosport, whose husband had been a Shipwright Officer to the ship. Apparently it was an occasional custom to give such a photograph to a crew member leaving the ship or as a gift at other times. Published by gracious permission of Her Majesty The Queen.)

Victoria and Albert (III).
(J & C McCutcheon Collection)

Elizabeth and the Duke of Kent were aboard for the Coronation Review of the Fleet. In July, the King and Queen, as a Coronation Visit, sailed from Stranraer to Belfast and back to Stranraer. In 1938, George VI with his brother, the Duke of Kent, witnessed Fleet exercises off Weymouth from *Victoria and Albert* (III). In 1939, with war a certainty, George VI, Queen Elizabeth, Princess Elizabeth and Princess Margaret embarked at Weymouth on 21 July to cruise to Torbay. From there they went on to visit the Royal Naval College at Dartmouth, then on to Cowes to visit Osborne House and thence to Portsmouth. On 9 August, King George VI voyaged to Weymouth Bay to inspect the Reserve Fleet, but used the royal barge to go aboard some of the ships. It was not realised at the time, but sadly this was the last occasion that a member of the Royal Family used this royal yacht.

During the First World War, it had been an accommodation ship for officers while docked in Portsmouth Dockyard. On 5 December 1939, not needed for active war service, the yacht was laid up at Portsmouth until 5 June 1942 when it was moored south of Whale Island. Here it was painted battleship grey and again used until 1945 as an accommodation ship for officers and men at HMS *Excellent*, a gunnery school. Fortunately, it survived the numerous air raids on the dockyard by the German Luftwaffe.

In 1946, *Victoria and Albert* (III) even underwent another refit, but its days as a royal yacht were over. Again having a black hull and, outwardly, a pre-war appearance, it underwent some sea-trials, but proved to be no longer seaworthy, mainly due to the condition of her boilers. So it was finally laid up at Portsmouth.

When the time came for them to be replaced by more modern ships, sailed yachts were in the main sold on, with the exception of *Britannia* (I). Steam-powered yachts were usually sold for scrap and eventually broken up, but before this work commenced certain artefacts, such as the Royal Coat of Arms or figurehead on the bows, would be removed. In 1954, furnishings, fittings and equipment were removed from *Victoria and Albert* (III). There had been a distinct royal stipulation that no items were to be taken from the ship as souvenirs. On the orders of Prince Philip, the two compass binnacles, previously on the *Royal George*, together with the ship's linen, silverware and glassware, were transferred to *Britannia*. One of the binnacles was put on the veranda deck. A sideboard and an antique mahogany bookcase from the King's study were put in *Britannia*'s anteroom, four sideboards carved in Chippendale style and two tables went into its State Dining Room, and a sofa and some armchairs furnished the Admiral's Suite. The Queen's bed on *Britannia* was covered with bed-linen from the royal yacht too.

The small silk White Ensign, referred to by Angela Fitzroy as associated with Captain Scott and given to George V by Admiral Evans in 1913, which had been hung in the reception lobby of *Victoria and Albert* (III), is now displayed in the anteroom in *Britannia*. An anchor, a fireplace and surround from the Queen's drawing room, a wardroom stove, two cupboards from the mizzenmast base and the Royal Arms and scroll from the stern were transferred to the Maritime Museum at Greenwich. The 'figurehead' (basically a scroll-head), a bell, some cannon, panelling and wall-lights went to the Royal Naval Barracks at Portsmouth. The main staircase and doors from the royal cabins went to HMS *Excellent*; some upper-deck gear, boat davits, etc., went to HMS *Royal Arthur*; and the ship's silver bell, given by the Merchant Taylor's Company, was returned to them.

On 1 December 1954, *Victoria and Albert* (III) left Portsmouth under tow to the Clyde Estuary where it was broken up by the British Iron & Steel Corporation at Faslane. What a tourist attraction it would have been today.

Britannia was the last royal yacht constructed for the personal use and official duties of Her Majesty Queen Elizabeth and other members of the Royal Family. However, since the end of the era of *Victoria and Albert* (III), the role for a royal yacht had changed. No longer was such a ship only in service for voyages around the British Isles, Europe and the Mediterranean. In the late twentieth century, it was now required to have the capability to sail worldwide to countries such as Australia, New Zealand and North America, to take part in important ceremonies and other functions, but also to host these with the monarch and Royal Family on board as well. This role was incorporated into the design of the new royal yacht. The keel for it was laid down at the John Brown & Co. Ltd shipyard on Clydebank in June 1952, although a replacement had been mooted during the early and then later years of the reign of George VI, but postponed due to the approaching war and the economic circumstances after it. A suggestion had been made that the German yacht, *Grille*, which was a rather grand and impressive-looking vessel, could become the 'new' British royal yacht, but this, not surprisingly, was turned down by George VI, although it had been an acquisitive practice acceptable to other countries to obtain a vessel for their Royal Family's use. For example, the 1,612-ton, diesel-engine-powered *Philante*, built in 1937 for Sir Thomas O. M. Sopwith, and requisitioned in 1939 for service in the Royal Navy, was bought in 1945 with donations from the Norwegian people and given to King Haakon to become the Norwegian royal yacht *Norge*. Even so, to convert the *Grille*, a second-hand ship, to a British royal yacht and in particular one of German origin too, would have looked cheapskate for a maritime country such as Britain to do in the eyes of the nautical world. A telegram was sent from the Admiralty on 4 February 1952, and confirmed by letter on the 5 February, to John Brown & Co. Ltd instructing them: 'to proceed forthwith with detailed design and construction on fair and reasonable price basis of hull machinery of vessel referred to in your letter McN/MK dated 24th November'.

The John Brown & Company Ltd's shipyard was an admirable choice, the passenger liners *Queen Mary* and *Queen Elizabeth*, two historic ships, were built there for Cunard. The designer of the royal yacht was Sir Victor Shepheard, Director of Naval Construction. Less than a year later, on 16 April 1953, *Britannia* was launched by Queen Elizabeth, accompanied by Prince Philip, and commissioned at sea in January 1954. The dimensions of this 5,862-gross-ton, single-funnelled, three-masted, twin-screw vessel was: an overall length of 412 feet 3 inches, a length between perpendiculars of 360 feet, a beam of 55 feet 7 inches, a load displacement of 4,715 tons, a mean draught at load displacement of 15 feet 7 inches, and a draught of 17 feet. Its two pairs of two-geared, 12,000-shaft-horsepower steam turbines, with two Foster Wheeler D-type boilers, reached a peak speed of 22.5 knots maximum, 21 knots continuous. The boilers, in a room adjoining the engine room, provided the steam that went via pipes to drive the turbines. The power they generated went through gearboxes to drive the propellers. There were also tanks for 210 tons of fresh water. Some of these water distillers had begun their naval career elsewhere, including the battleship HMS *Queen Elizabeth*, which saw service in the Royal Navy in the First World War. Three turbo-steam generators provided the required electricity throughout the ship. Electric power was also available in an emergency from a diesel generator that had formerly been on HM submarine *Vampire*.

The cruising range of *Britannia* was 2,196 miles at 20 knots, 2,553 miles at 18 knots. Over the years, these engines steamed some 1,087,623 nautical miles. Fuel oil capacity was 330 tons for a range of 2,000 miles at 20 knots with another 20 tons of oil for the 40-foot-long royal barge and several smaller motor boats on board. With the addition of auxiliary tanks the fuel oil capacity was increased to 490 tons. The oil originally used was furnace fuel oil (FFO), but in a 1983 refit, which included the installation of new satellite communications, a new sewage system and new soot scrubbers, the oil was changed from FFO to diesel fuel.

The hull of *Britannia* was fully rivetted, but smooth due to the application of a special foundation layer followed by six coats of paint. It was painted blue instead of the traditional black of former steam royal yachts. This colour was chosen by the Queen and Prince Philip to be in keeping with *Bluebottle*, the racing yacht that had been one of the wedding gifts they received in 1948. The hull was also partially reinforced and instead of three-bladed propellers it had a four-bladed variety, so the ship was virtually vibration-free. Its retractable stabilisers were also effective in rough seas.

The ancient tradition of adorning the bows with the Royal Badge, the Royal Coat of Arms, was continued on *Britannia*. Some earlier royal yachts had displayed carved wooden figureheads instead of, or in addition to, the Royal Arms. The main superstructure was white, the funnel was yellow. The various boat davits were white; but the hull of each of the two motor boats, the two jolly boats, the royal barge and the 'activity boat', used to take the Royal Family ashore for private visits, picnics, etc., was the same blue as the hull. The air-conditioned 12.5-metre-long royal barge, with its two 125-horsepower engines, with a maximum speed of 20 knots, was built by Camper Nicholson at Southampton in 1964. This barge, when it had royalty on board, would be escorted by one of the fast motor boats in a close aft position.

Britannia's three hollow white masts varied in height; the foremast was 133 feet, the mainmast was 139 feet 3 inches and the mizzenmast was 118 feet 10 inches. At the foremast truck, when the Queen was on board, was flown the Admiralty Flag (red with a horizontal gold foul anchor), the badge of office of the Lord High

The passing away of the old and arrival of the new. The Royal Yacht *Britannia* coming into harbour at Portsmouth as preparations are made to tow the former Royal Yacht *Victoria and Albert* (III) to a ship-breaker's yard. (*Portsmouth News*, Hampshire)

The *Britannia*, February 1954.

The Royal Yacht *Britannia*. (J & C McCutcheon Collection)

Admiral. At the mainmast truck, the Royal Standard was flown. At the mizzenmast truck, the Union Flag, as the symbol of an Admiral of the Fleet, was flown. If the Sovereign was not on board, but other members of the Royal Family were, there were variations from these flag arrangements, notably the use of their personal standards. The Union Flag was flown on the bow's jackstaff and the White Ensign on the stern ensign staff. When royalty was not on board, the Admiral's Flag was flown at the mizzenmast. In the Royal Navy, it was the practice to keep these flags flying by night only on the royal yacht. When in harbour with the Sovereign aboard, Royal Navy ships accompanying the yacht would be 'dressed overall' from morning colours to sunset, but when they were sailing with the royal yacht, they just wore the masthead flags. When visiting overseas ports and during foreign island cruises, the *Britannia* was also frequently 'dressed overall' too, but not while at sea.

Forty-three different patterned flags were used in 'dressing ship overall', but there was no special message related in the manner they were flown. During the long naval career of *Britannia*, it was inevitable that occasions would arise when the ship had to pass under low bridges. To cope with this eventuality, the upper 20 feet of the mainmast, with the radio aerial, was hinged. Incidentally, the historical flags referred to were not the only ones *Britannia* carried. Some 2,000 different national and other flags, necessary when visiting countries worldwide, were in the flag lockers.

The operational part of *Britannia* was forward of the mainmast, comprising the bridge, wheelhouse and flag deck. On the bridge, the nerve centre of the ship, the decisions were taken for its control. The plotting of the routes for *Britannia* when on voyages took place in the chart house behind the bridge. On the flag deck, also rear of the bridge, contact was made with other ships by using signal flags hoisted on ropes. Alternatively, Morse code messages were sent via the deck's signal lights.

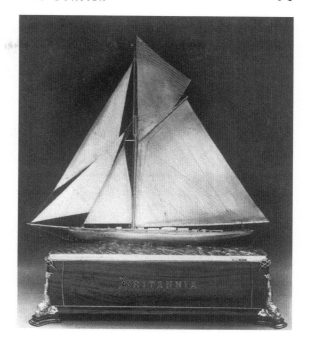

A model of the *Britannia*.
(J & C McCutcheon Collection)

Royal Yacht *Britannia* at Portsmouth,
28 August 1972.
(J & C McCutcheon Collection)

To reduce the amount and volume of noise when the Sovereign and Royal Family were aboard, orders, instead of being shouted or even loudly verbally stated, were usually given by hand sign actions. On *Victoria and Albert* (III), the crew working on the decks had to do so as silently as possible. Orders for tasks or what to do were usually signalled, sometimes with small flags. One early method was to use hand-held wooden pads coloured red on one side for 'Stop', and green on the other side for 'Hoist', 'Lower' or 'Go'. Below decks communication could be by telephone. I was told by a former yachtsman that some of the royal yachts were initially carpeted on their upper decks also to encourage silence. Should it come on to rain hard, the carpeting would soon be wet and soggy, so the crew on the decks and any off duty were summoned to take up the carpeting immediately and stow it to avoid this happening. This is also referred to in respect of *Victoria and Albert* (III). The crew also wore soft-soled footwear, a sort of plimsoll, on deck to avoid noisy footsteps. Tasks aft on the *Britannia* had to be completed by 9 a.m., but should a crew member on duty need to go aft later, he did so via the main and lower deck's passageways.

When under way on a voyage, an Officer of the Watch would be in charge, supported by a lookout and signalman, who were in contact via two voice pipes with the helmsman steering by means of the ship's wheel on the deck below. Also on the deck below the bridge, was the royal bridge from where the Queen, Prince Philip and sometimes other members of the Royal Family would return waves to people waving to them on the shore, piers and harbour sides, as the ship passed by. In the wheelhouse below was the helmsman, assisted by two other crew members who, when under way, had the task of operating the brass telegraphs on either side of the ship's wheel. These, by means of mechanical rod gearing, were in contact with the engine room five decks below, communicating orders to control the engines regarding the progress of the ship.

In its early years *Britannia* had on its compass platform, which also incorporated the bridge, chart house and flag deck, two three-pounder cannons that were used to fire salutes. These were eventually removed because the gun smoke tended to discolour the white paintwork. The sound they made was also considered too loud for the purpose, so the escorting Royal Navy ships fired salutes when required instead.

In recognition of his rank and responsibility, the Admiral was accommodated in the roomy, air-conditioned Admiral's Suite on the shelter deck. This comprised a day cabin furnished with a long table, chairs, sofa, two armchairs, occasional table, writing desk, cabinets, pedestal lamp and a fireplace, for working and, when necessary, eating meals. Also it could be used for entertaining his guests on special occasions. There was also a sleeping cabin that housed wardrobes for his uniforms, etc., plus a bathroom. Behind this suite, and sharing a corridor and landing with it, were the senior officers' cabins. Each contained the furniture and artefacts that an officer would require, both on and off duty, plus sleeping quarters with a space-saving sofa bed. The junior officers' cabins were a deck below, on the upper deck. The officers' wardroom was also on the upper deck, behind the junior officers' cabins. Here the ship's officers dined in considerable formal splendour, as befit their ranks, dressed accordingly in Red Sea Rig – black trousers, white shirt, cummerbund and leather shoes. Prior to dining, drinks were available in an equally comfortably furnished anteroom, adjoining the wardroom, wherein the officers relaxed in various ways. The loyal toast was made at the conclusion of dinner. In the wardroom was a silver bowl with engraved panels showing some of the earlier royal yachts that had been given by officers of *Victoria and Albert* (III). Other accommodation on the main deck was the Warrant Officers' and Chief

Petty Officers' mess and their sleeping quarters, the Petty Officers' and Royal Marine Sergeants' mess and sleeping quarters, the Royal Marines' living and sleeping quarters, and the 'barracks' for the twenty-six Royal Marine Bandsmen. There was also the important Mail Office for the daily reception and despatching of official mail and the officers' and crew's mail. Not forgetting a NAAFI shop selling items for the basic requirements of those aboard. It continues today in *Britannia*'s retirement, but now selling to visitors on the ship.

The health of all those on board when at sea was catered for by the sick bay on the main deck. This had a doctor's consulting room and, if it became necessary, use of an adjoining tiled-floor operating theatre. On the same deck, important to ensure a spotlessly uniformed ship's complement, was a large tiled-floor laundry, with washing machines, driers, steam presses and its own permanent crew, who sometimes had to deal with a phenomenal quantity of clothing items, especially before and after official events, working around the clock.

The three galleys supplying food to everyone aboard were on the upper deck. These comprised a 'royal galley' for the Royal Family and royal household, an 'officers galley' for the ship's officers, and a 'ship's galley' for the crew. The food for the officers and crew was prepared by the ship's naval catering staff, but Buckingham Palace chefs joined *Britannia* to cater for the Royal Family and royal household when the Queen was on board. To the rear of the mainmast were the air-conditioned royal apartments, designed by architect Sir Hugh Casson, and the State Rooms. On the shelter deck was the Queen's bedroom and Prince Philip's bedroom, and on the upper deck was the Queen's sitting room, Prince Philip's sitting room, the State Dining Room and State Drawing Room with an anteroom.

The Queen, with Prince Philip, was equally and closely involved with the design of *Britannia* as was Queen Victoria in respect of the *Victoria and Albert* (III), the rooms and contents of which had been designed in large part by her beloved Prince Albert. Unlike Queen Victoria's vessel, however, this new royal yacht was to be much more than a ship that only travelled to Europe and around the British Isles with the Royal Family and other European royalty. As the Queen stated: '*Britannia* is to be at times the home of my husband and myself and of our family.'

Nearest to the stern is the large State Drawing Room, where the Royal Family met to relax, also serving as the chief reception room. On the floor are a silver-grey carpet and two large Persian rugs. The grey fireplace has an electric fire and above it is a large oil painting of *Britannia* by J. A. Wilcox. The walls are cream and complement the floral-patterned covered sofas and armchairs. There is also a Walmar baby grand piano bolted to the floor, used by some of the Royal Family to entertain family and guests. In this room there is also a small table on gimbals (a device for suspending an object so that it remains level, however much its support is inclined by the rolling of the ship). The table, designed by Prince Albert, had been in his dressing room on *Victoria and Albert* (II) and later in the King's writing room on *Victoria and Albert* (III). The satinwood desk also came from *Victoria and Albert* (II) and was used by Queen Victoria. Adjoining the drawing room was a smaller anteroom reached by folding back some separating mahogany doors and used by the Royal Family and guests to gather for drinks before going to the State Dining Room. It is furnished with a plain sofa, armchairs and easy chairs, also standing on a silver-grey carpet. From this anteroom more folding mahogany doors open onto a foyer-style area at the foot of the grand staircase, which leads to the shelter deck; both the stairs and foyer are entirely silver-grey carpeted.

On the starboard side of the grand staircase, between the State Drawing Room and State Dining Room, was the Queen's sitting room. It is moss-green carpeted

The royal homecoming on board *Britannia*.

and furnished with armchair, settee, writing desk and chair, and also a grey, oblong fireplace with an electric fire. This was her private room for relaxing, but also where meetings were held with her press and private secretaries and where she attended to the official correspondence despatched to her, even aboard *Britannia*, in whatever area it was sailing or visiting. On the port side of the grand staircase was Prince Philip's sitting room, similarly purposed. It is silver-grey carpeted, but the walls, however, have teak panelling. Both sitting rooms had telephone links connected to the offices of their secretaries on the main deck.

Beyond the grand staircase and entered by two separate pairs of doors was the State Dining Room, the largest room on *Britannia*. Again silver-grey carpeted, the walls are white with gold trim. The centrepiece was the long thirty-two-seater, five-section, D-ended dining table with Hepplewhite-style chairs, used for the numerous State Banquets held there. On the walls and in the alcoves are displayed many of the gifts given to the Queen and Prince Philip on their worldwide official visits. It was also used for Royal Family informal dining, a church for Sunday worship and on occasions a cinema. The dining room was, however, reassembled at Frogmore, Windsor, on the instructions of Prince Philip, to be used for meetings, after the decommissioning of *Britannia*.

The grand staircase and a lift led up to the shelter deck and the Royal Family's four bedrooms. The Queen's bedroom on the starboard side has wall-to-wall, silver-grey carpeting on the floor, pale cream walls and the usual 1950s-style bedroom furniture, plus a built-in desk. What is immediately noticeable is the charming foliate design of the curtains, armchairs and bed cover. Above the bed are an equally impressive large silk panel and two narrow side panels similarly embroidered with foliage, flowers and butterflies. This was designed in 1953 by Joan Nicholson, a British designer. The background material is of French ivory silk, the embroidery on it is by the members of the Royal School of Needlework. Nearby on the same deck was the Queen's maids' room and the wardrobe rooms that housed the Queen's clothes, jewellery and other accessories. Also on the starboard side was Prince Philip's bedroom, similarly carpeted but with plain walls, the usual bedroom furniture, plus a desk and wardrobe. On the port side are another two bedrooms, one of which had the only double bed on *Britannia*. These were used by various Royal Family members. The bedroom floors were raised two feet higher than the outside deck, partly to accommodate the design of the rooms underneath them, but also, because of their height, making it impossible for passers-by on the outside deck from seeing into the bedroom windows. A silver-grey carpeted lobby or vestibule leads from these bedrooms towards the stern and into the sun lounge. On the vestibule's pale walls hang photographs of past and present Royal Family members aboard royal yachts and centrally a portrait of Lord Nelson. The comfortably furnished sun lounge was totally private for the Royal Family's use. In its wood-panelled walls is a row of large, long window, giving a view over the verandah deck to the sea and beyond. Two doors open from the sun lounge onto the broad area of this deck for informal and sometimes State occasions.

When aboard, the Royal Family were served from their own galley, with its own chinaware and silver pantries, the kitchen having tiled floors, stainless-steel surfaces and electric cookers.

On the aft of the main deck, below the upper deck, were a special guest suite, the Ladies-in-Waiting sitting room, and the Royal Household and guest cabins. More cabins for Royal Household staff were on the aft lower deck, adjoining the Royal Household mess. Amidships, on the shelter deck, perhaps rather surprisingly, there was a garage for the Queen's Rolls-Royce Phantom V, which was used to convey her and Prince Philip on land during foreign visits. On family holiday cruises, it alternatively housed a Land Rover.

Also on board were the royal valet's bedroom, the maids' sitting room, a strong room, the Master of the Household's cabin, the equerry's sitting room, a baggage room, extra blanket, linen and chinaware stores, wine and beer stores, extra bathrooms and showers, the yachtsmen's mess, the stewards' and cooks' mess, the stokers' mess, the Chief Petty Officers' cabin, a cold room, an air-conditioning plant, the engineers', shipwrights' and joiners' workshops, a paint shop, a barber's shop, a telephone exchange using radio telephone, and also four transmitters, and encoding and decoding equipment. Thus the *Britannia* at sea was a complete, self-contained floating entity.

In the 1950s, the opinion of a percentage of the British public may have been that it would be a self-indulgence to build a ship only for the use of the Royal Family. Therefore, from the start of planning, the royal yacht was designed with the intention that it should, if the need arose, be quickly convertible into an alternative use, such as a hospital ship. Originally, the scheme was to use the State Dining Room as sick officers' quarters, the State Drawing Room as an isolation ward, the wine cellar as a medical store, and to strengthen the verandah deck to bear the weight of a helicopter bringing in and evacuating casualties. However, in 1982, at the beginning of the Falklands War, when the Flag Officer Royal Yachts expected to receive orders to sail to the South Atlantic to perform this vital role as a casualty evacuation ship, this detachment was not agreed to for two reasons. One was a logistics problem. *Britannia* would be the only ship in the task force to the Falkland Islands, apart from the aircraft carrier *Hermes*, that used FFO fuel and there could be problems with refuelling. Secondly, it was thought the royal yacht would be a priority target for the Argentinian Air Force to attack, even if repainted. If it had been damaged or sunk, this could have been used as a propaganda coup by Argentina. Even so, the Flag Officer, officers and crew at that time were deeply disappointed not to be allowed to perform this role. This disappointment was partially salved in 1986, when *Britannia* was sailing in the vicinity of South Yemen on a voyage to Australia. When civil war broke out in South Yemen, British civilian personnel in the region had to be collected by boats from *Britannia*. On arriving on board, after receiving food and refreshment, the 1,068 grateful rescued of various nationalities spent their time in the State Drawing Room, anteroom and dormitories, until they could be safely transferred ashore elsewhere.

When the Queen was on board, the *Britannia* never sailed alone, but had an escort. It would be Trinity House yacht which had the 500-year-old right to lead a royal yacht in pilotage waters. In later years, Trinity House only exercised this right on ceremonial occasions. At sea, *Britannia* was usually preceded by one or two Royal Navy ships. On a visit to a foreign country, as *Britannia* drew close to a country's territorial waters or port, the host nation's ships became escorts and the Royal Navy ships retreated to an aft position. If not docking, *Britannia* dropped anchor and raised signal flags. The royal barge may then have been lowered over the side and a companionway lowered into position to allow the disembarking of royalty and any other notables to transport them ashore.

The highlight of the Queen's year, which was looked forward to, was the annual holiday cruise among the Hebrides. Prior to this, the royal yacht, with the Queen, Prince Philip and other members of the Royal Family, European royalty and other guests aboard, would attend the Cowes Week regatta, so maintaining the royal tradition of attendance at this event. Some of the Royal Family would also take part in the yacht racing. Following this, *Britannia* sailed north to the Western Isles of Scotland. Despite there being the necessary full complement of officers and crew, some of her personal staff and Royal Household were also aboard. The mere isolation of the ship and cruise afforded the Queen a week or so away from the routine of her life and glare of publicity to enjoy the environment of the area she loves. It was a tradition as well, during the cruise, to anchor for the day off the Pentland Firth at Scrabster and for the Royal Family to lunch with the Queen Mother at her home, the Castle of Mey. This allowed further relaxation in the castle and its grounds, and also to partake in afternoon tea, after which the Queen and Royal Family returned to *Britannia* and sailed for Aberdeen and finally reached Balmoral, where, in the meantime, the rest of the Royal Household would

The Royal Yacht *Britannia*.

have arrived by road. The departure from the Castle of Mey was, by tradition, marked, as the light faded, by a display of fireworks fired from the battlements and with white sheets being waved from the ramparts. *Britannia* acknowledged this by firing a battery of flares as a salute to the Queen Mother's send-off.

The forty-four-year career of *Britannia* included some 700 overseas visits and covered a wide range of tasks and events. On 1 May 1954, the Queen embarked on the royal yacht for the first time, not in Britain, but surprisingly at Torbruk, Libya, en route to Malta, Gibraltar, and then returning to London. This was followed by Prince Philip visiting Canada, Quebec and Montreal, and then back to Aberdeen.

First and foremost in the career of *Britannia* were the worldwide State visits undertaken by the Queen and Prince Philip to Commonwealth and other countries, some celebratory, others courteous in purpose; sometimes receptions were also held aboard for guest kings and queens, crown princes, presidents, rulers, prime ministers, diplomats and other notables.

Being on *Britannia* was also an ideal way of gaining privacy away from the media for four royal honeymooners. Princess Margaret and Anthony Armstrong-Jones went to the Caribbean in 1960; Princess Anne and Captain Mark Phillips also sailed to the Caribbean in 1973; Prince Charles and Diana, Lady Spencer, toured the Mediterranean in 1981; and Prince Andrew and Lady Sarah Ferguson went to the Azores in 1987.

From 1968, the ship was also used successfully to promote British trade and industry. Representatives of various consortiums could meet aboard in favourable circumstances with their relevant opposite numbers in the regions visited and contracts would ensue.

Other miscellaneous tasks for the vessel included taking part, with the Queen on board, in a Review of the NATO Fleet in May 1969, sailing to Dover with the Queen Mother for her installation as Lord Warden of the Cinque Ports, and travelling to San Nazaire with veterans on the fortieth anniversary of the successful wartime raid on that French port. *Britannia* also rendezvoused off Southampton with the liner *Queen Elizabeth* (II) returning from the Falklands War zone, so the Queen could welcome home the survivors from HMS *Ardent*, *Coventry* and *Antelope*. In 1959, *Britannia* was present at the opening of the St Lawrence Seaway, the Canada–USA project linking the Great Lakes with the Atlantic Ocean. On this occasion the Queen and Prince Philip were aboard, together with President and Mrs Dwight Eisenhower of the USA, and the Prime Minister and Mrs John Diefenbaker of Canada. Another royal duty was taking Prince Philip on a tour of the Antarctic in 1956.

The final official visit of *Britannia* sailing from Portsmouth to a foreign port was made on 20 January 1997, on a trip to Hong Kong to be present at the handing over of the British colony to China on 30 June. Following the ceremony of lowering the Union Jack, it sailed from the former colony's harbour conveying Prince Charles and Chris Patten, its last governor, back to Britain, arriving at Portsmouth on 1 August. This was followed six days later by attendance at Cowes Week and, following this, the cruise to the Western Isles with the Queen and Royal Family.

Paradoxically, although it had been a former Labour Prime Minister, Clement Attlee, of the 1945 elected Labour Government, who had, in late 1950, put in train plans for *Britannia*, it was a Labour government, that of Prime Minister Tony Blair, which had decided not to refit this royal yacht for further use, nor even commission the building of a replacement. The estimated cost of £80 million proposed by the Ministry of Defence was too much for them, despite all the

Royal Yacht *Britannia* anchored at Nanaimo, Vancouver Island, March 1983, during a visit of the Queen and Prince Philip to British Columbia, Canada. In the foreground passing the bows is one of the famous bathtubs 'sailed' in the region's Bathtubs races, some of them smaller than this example and bath size. (Peirson's Photography, Nanaimo, B.C., Canada)

The *Britannia* at sail. (J & C McCutcheon Collection)

The Royal Barge attached to *Britannia*, used to bring members of the Royal Family ashore. (J & C McCutcheon Collection)

The Trinity House Yacht *Patricia* and Royal Yacht *Britannia* at a NATO review, 18 August 1969. (J & C McCutcheon Collection)

benefits a royal yacht brought in trade and prestige to Britain. It proved to be an unbelievable decision in the context of later capital expenditure by that government, particularly among the rulers of Middle Eastern countries. Lesser countries than ours could afford such a ship. Great Britain was less great in their eyes and others worldwide.

The decision stood. *Britannia* sailed from Portsmouth on 20 October 1997 to visit six major ports as part of a goodbye tour of Britain. On 21 November 1997, flying its paying-off pennant, the ship sailed from London, arriving the next day at Portsmouth, its decommissioning port. On 11 December, the official ceremony of decommissioning took place with the Queen, Prince Philip and twelve others of the Royal Family present for what was a sad occasion for all attending. Also present were 2,200 former royal yacht officers and yachtsmen crew with their families. The last deed was that of the Band of Her Majesty's Royal Marines, Portsmouth, who, as they marched away, played 'Auld Lang Syne' and saluted *Britannia*. The maritime and royal career of Britain's last royal yacht was finished.

As the Queen aptly commented:

> Looking back over forty-four years we can all reflect with pride and gratitude upon this great ship which has served the country, the Royal Navy and my family with such distinction. *Britannia* has provided magnificent support to us throughout this time, playing such an important role in the history of the second half of this century.

However, what was to be done with so illustrious a ship? Sell it to the ruler or government of a foreign, wealthier country? Perhaps to a company in the cruise liner business? There would have been numerous bidders for it at £250,000. Or send it to a ship-breaker overseas? The protests from all and sundry in Britain would have been deafening. Scuttling it, perhaps off the Western Isles in deep water? Again the protests would have been so loud and strong that no purpose had been found for its last years. Fortunately, *Britannia* did not have this ignominious end or that of going to the ship-breakers. It was put up for sale, but with conditions for who or what bought it. The desired suitable purchaser was one that could and would preserve the ship and use it in a fashion acceptable and accessible to the British public.

In April 1998, the Labour Government announced that the offer of Forth Ports PLC had been chosen as it intended to make *Britannia* part of its scheme to regenerate its port of Leith, Edinburgh. The Ministry of Defence transferred the ownership of *Britannia* on 29 April 1998 to a registered charity, the Royal Yacht Britannia Trust, which was charged with preserving and maintaining the ship. On 5 May 1998, *Britannia* arrived at Edinburgh to be dry-docked, then refurbished to make it more easily accessible to the public, for which it was opened on 19 October 1998. Until September 2001, *Britannia* was docked in the Western Harbour, but was then transferred next to the Ocean Terminal at Leith, which is its permanent home. As with *Cutty Sark* at Greenwich, and other historic vessels still surviving in harbours and maritime museums, *Britannia* is thankfully included in the Core Collection of the National Register of Historic Vessels. Reflecting on this forward-thinking, it is tragic that the Core Collection was not in existence in earlier years so that some of the former graceful royal yachts would also now be preserved.

The *Brittania* at anchor, 1997. (J & C McCutcheon Collection)

'TEMPORARY' ROYAL YACHTS

Situations occasionally arose where, for one or more of a variety of reasons, no royal yacht was available to take the Sovereign or members of the Royal Family on an official, long-distance destination voyage. Perhaps it was being refitted at this time, or in use elsewhere at the same time as it was suddenly unexpectedly required for such duty. To meet this contingency the Admiralty converted one of its Royal Navy ships for the purpose, or even chartered a notable, commercial passenger liner.

In 1869, *Victoria and Albert* (II) was unavailable, after being found to be rotten amidships and in need of repair in 1868. A ship was required to convey Edward, Prince of Wales, and Princess Alexandra to Egypt to take part in the opening of the Suez Canal ceremony. So the Admiralty impressed into service the HMS *Ariadne*, a Royal Navy frigate which was altered during several weeks in Malta Dockyard. The guns were removed, ports converted to windows for the Royal Suite and various other comforts added for the royal party, which included Prince Louis of Battenberg, later to be 1st Marquess of Milford Haven and the First Sea Lord, but serving at this time as a junior midshipman on HMS *Ariadne*.

They embarked at Trieste on 27 January 1869 to commence the voyage to Egypt. After attending several functions, including an Egyptian steamer cruise on the River Nile, the Prince and Princess of Wales embarked on Khedive Ismail Pasha of Egypt's steam yacht, *Mahroussa*, which had a long career from 1865 until 1975, for a voyage from Port Said to Alexandria and a banquet on the way there. The interior of *Mahroussa* was sumptuous with marble staircases and fittings, parquet floors, luxurious furnishings, silver candelabra and Sevres chinaware on the tables.

Prince Louis later described the scene when *Mahroussa* began the voyage:

Suddenly, as the ship rounded the breakwater, she gave two or three very heavy rolls. The whole of the heavy gilt chairs on one side slid away to leeward with their occupants along the parquet floor to the ship's side while the candelabra and fruit dishes fell over with a great clatter. At the next roll the chairs on the other side slid away, leaving the bare table deserted. At the same time piles of plates which stood on the marble consoles along each wall crashed down in two avalanches; most of the lights also went out. Needless to say, the Khedive's servants were sprawling on the floor, mixed up with the guests and the general wreckage. A few minutes later the ship was once more as steady as a church.

Probably thankful to be back on *Ariadne*, the Prince and Princess of Wales continued their voyage, visiting Constantinople and Sebastopol, returning through the Bosphorus and Dardanelles to Piraeus. Here King George of Greece, Princess Alexandra's brother, joined the 'royal yacht' for lunch. This was followed by sailing to Corfu to visit Queen Olga of Greece and finally to Brindisi, Italy, where the prince and princess disembarked to return overland to England. HMS *Ariadne* was then restored to service as a Royal Navy frigate.

From October 1875 to May 1876, HMS *Serapis*, an Indian troopship, was used as a royal yacht for the official tour to India of Edward, Prince of Wales. In 1901, the 6,910-ton Orient Line passenger liner *Ophir*, built by Robert Napier & Co. on the Clyde in 1891, was chartered to take the Prince and Princess of Wales, later King George V and Queen Mary, to Australia to open the first Commonwealth Parliament at Melbourne on 9 May 1901. Its dimensions were: a length of 482 feet, a beam of 52 feet 6 inches and a draught 37 feet. Several alterations were made to the liner, notably to the accommodation. It was repainted white, its two funnels painted yellow. Leaving Portsmouth on 16 March, *Ophir* was led by the Trinity House yacht *Irene*, followed by *Alberta* with Edward VII and Queen Alexandra aboard, plus an escort of torpedo-boat destroyers. *Alberta* eventually reduced speed and went astern and *Ophir* continued on its way, taking the royal couple to visit Ceylon, New Zealand, Tasmania, South Africa and Canada. It arrived back at Portsmouth on 1 November 1901, being met and led into the Solent by the Trinity House *Irene* and *Victoria and Albert* (III) with Edward VII and Queen Alexandra aboard. From October 1905 to April 1906, the battleship HMS *Renown* was used to take the Prince and Princess of Wales on a tour to India. In 1908, the battlecruiser HMS *Indomitable* was used to take the Prince of Wales to Quebec on the 150th anniversary of General Wolfe landing in Canada.

In October 1910, the Union Castle liner *Balmoral Castle* was used to take the Duke and Duchess of Connaught and Princess Patricia of Connaught to South Africa to open the first Parliament of the Union of South Africa. The Duke also laid the foundation stone of Cape University. The Royal Party embarked on the *Balmoral Castle* leaving Durban on 3 December 1910 for England.

In 1911, it was again decided it would be preferable to use a commercial liner as a royal yacht to convey George V and Queen Mary to India for the Coronation Durbar at Delhi. The P&O liner *Medina* was chartered and modifications made to it. These included adding accommodation and a third mast to carry the correct flags. The liner was painted white, with yellow funnels, now also displaying the White Ensign as HMS *Medina*. On 11 November, the now HMS *Medina* sailed from Portsmouth en route via Gibraltar, the Suez Canal, Aden, and Bombay, for the triumphant Durbar in India. On 10 January 1912, the King and Queen re-embarked at Bombay, arriving back at Spithead on 4 February 1912, having been delayed at Malta for three days due to a fouled propeller. Sadly *Medina* was sunk off Start Point, Devon, by a German submarine torpedo on 28 April 1917.

In 1919, battlecruiser HMS *Renown* was chosen to take Edward, Prince of Wales, to Canada on a 'thank you' mission for that country's support to Britain in the First World War. Sailing from Portsmouth on 5 August it arrived at Newfoundland on 11 August and at Quebec on 21 August. After Edward had toured Canada and the USA, HMS *Renown* returned to Portsmouth with its royal passenger on 1 December. On 16 March 1920, HMS *Renown* again sailed from Portsmouth with Prince Edward aboard, this time en route to the West Indies, Panama Canal, Honolulu, and across the Pacific Ocean to Australia and New Zealand, arriving back at Portsmouth 11 October 1920.

The *Ophir*.

The *Ophir* in Dry Dock,
Halifax, Nova Scotia.
(J & C McCutcheon
Collection)

The *Medina*. (J & C McCutcheon Collection)

HM King George V and Queen Mary on board HMS *Medina* with members of their suite and the officers of the ship. (J & C McCutcheon Collection)

The Engineer Captain and Engineer Officers on HMS *Medina*. (J & C McCutcheon Collection)

The 250 WOs, POs, NCOs and men of HMS *Medina* at dinner on 6 February 1912 after the thanksgiving service at St Paul's Cathedral for their Majesties safe return from India. (J & C McCutcheon Collection)

The Queen's sitting room on HMS *Medina*. (J & C McCutcheon Collection)

The reading room on HMS *Medina*. (J & C McCutcheon Collection)

The Queen's bedroom on HMS *Medina*. (J & C McCutcheon Collection)

The *Medina* in Greenock Docks. (J & C McCutcheon Collection)

The *Medina* on an outward journey to Durban, November 1911. (J & C McCutcheon Collection)

A model of the *Medina*. (J & C McCutcheon Collection)

Left: A superb bow shot of the *Medina*. (J & C McCutcheon Collection)

Below: The *Medina* at sail. (J & C McCutcheon Collection)

In December 1920, the Duke of Connaught sailed on the battleship HMS *Malaya* to India to open the Provincial Legislative Council. On 26 October 1921, HMS *Renown*, still in use as a royal yacht, sailed from Portsmouth with Edward, Prince of Wales, and Lieutenant Lord Louis Mountbatten to Gibraltar, Malta, Port Said, Suez, Aden and Bombay, for the Prince to tour India for four months. Leaving Karachi on 17 March 1922, HMS *Renown* set off for Japan, Ceylon, the Federated Malay States, Hong Kong, arriving at Yokohama, Japan, on 12 April 1922. It later left Kagoshima on 9 May 1922 for the Philippine Islands, Labuan, Brunei, Penang, Ceylon, Suez and Gibraltar, arriving at Plymouth on 20 June 1922.

In March 1925, the battlecruiser HMS *Repulse* took the Prince of Wales on an African and South American tour, returning in October.

HMS *Renown* was considered an impressive success as a royal yacht and was chosen again in January 1927, this time to take Albert George, Duke of York, and his wife, Elizabeth, Duchess of York, to Australia to open the Commonwealth Parliament at Canberra, then to visit New Zealand. It was not an incident-free return voyage. While crossing the Indian Ocean a serious fire occurred in the boiler room and rapidly got close to the main fuel tanks. In an earlier violent storm the ship's lifeboats had been damaged or destroyed and the sea was still very rough. Surprisingly, the *Renown*'s escort was three days' sailing away and unable to effect any help or rescue. Fortunately, the desperate situation was brought under control.

Two more passenger liners used as royal yachts were the *Empress of Australia* and the *Empress of Britain*. The *Empress of Australia* (ex-*Empress of China*, ex-*Tirpitz*) was built in 1914 for the Canadian Pacific Railway Co. In 1939, George VI and Queen Elizabeth sailed to Canada and the USA on this chartered RMAS liner, arriving at Quebec on 17 May. The purpose of this visit was basically to encourage support for Britain should a war begin. The return voyage was made on the *Empress of Britain*, arriving at Southampton on 21 June 1939. This liner was built in 1931 for the Canadian Pacific Railway Co. (Canadian Pacific Steamship Co.). Off the coast of Ireland in October 1940, it was attacked by German bombers and set on fire, but taken in tow, only to be sunk the following day by a torpedo from a German submarine, U-32.

In the winter of 1947, HMS *Vanguard* conveyed George VI, Queen Elizabeth, Princess Elizabeth (our present Queen) and Princess Margaret to South Africa, the first visit to that country by a reigning British monarch and also with the intention of being a 'thank you' for their aid during the Second World War. It was during this voyage to South Africa that Princess Elizabeth and Princess Margaret were inducted in the Crossing the Line (Equator) Ceremony. The *Vanguard* and Royal Family arrived back in Portsmouth on 12 May 1948.

The Shaw Savill ship SS *Gothic* was chartered from the owners for £40,000 a month charter fee by the Admiralty, and then converted to be a passenger ship for use by Queen Elizabeth and Prince Philip for the Queen's Commonwealth Tour in late 1953 and early 1954. Alterations included painting the original black hull white, with a white superstructure and a yellow and black funnel. In the Queen's drawing room on the *Gothic* were a 'ship's wheel' mirror and several wall lights that were eventually transferred to the Queen's sitting room on *Britannia*.

Due to the former royal yacht *Victoria and Albert* (III) not being in a fit condition to undertake such a sea duty and its successor, *Britannia*, still under construction, another vessel was required for Queen Elizabeth's use at the Coronation Naval Review at Spithead on 15 June 1953. The ship used by the Queen to Review the Fleet was the 'yacht' or 'Despatch Vessel' of the Commander-in-Chief, Mediterranean, Malta, the frigate HMS *Surprise* (ex-*Loch Carron*, ex-*Gerrans Bay*).

The homecoming of the Duke and Duchess of York, leaving HMS *Renown* after their Empire Tour. They are followed by the Prince of Wales, Prince Henry and Prince George. (J & C McCutcheon Collection)

HMS *Renown* dressed. (J & C McCutcheon Collection)

HMS *Renown* in the upper chambers of Gatun Lock, Panama Canal, 30 March 1920.
(J & C McCutcheon Collection)

HMS *Renown* at Chagres river crossing and entering the Gaillard Cut, 30 March 1920.
(J & C McCutcheon Collection)

The *Empress of Australia* at Portsmouth. (J & C McCutcheon Collection)

The *Empress of Australia* at Portsmouth. (J & C McCutcheon Collection)

Right & below:
A dinner menu to commemorate the Atlantic voyage of King George and Queen Elizabeth to visit Canada. The journey was made on the *Empress of Australia.*
(J & C McCutcheon Collection)

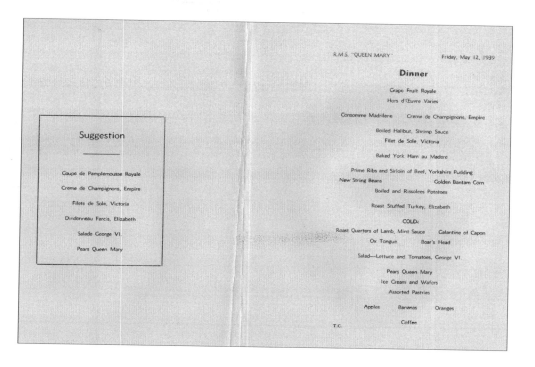

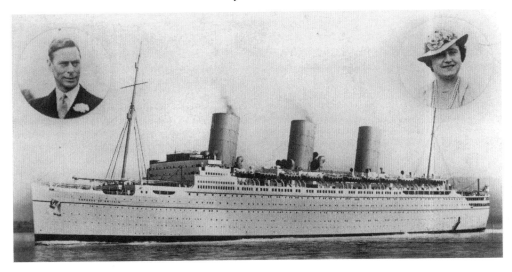

Canadian Pacific liner *Empress of Britain*. (J & C McCutcheon Collection)

HMS *Vanguard* was a temporary royal yacht for King George VI, Queen Elizabeth, Princess Elizabeth (our present Queen) and Princess Margaret for a trip to South Africa in 1947. (J & C McCutcheon Collection)

The *Gothic* as a Royal Yacht.

The Royal drawing room aboard the *Gothic* where receptions were held. (J & C McCutcheon Collection)

It had been laid down in 1944 at Smith's Dock and launched on 14 March 1945. Temporary conversions for the Review included the fitting of a long deck towards the stern for entertaining purposes, etc., removing a gun mount and constructing a glass-enclosed saluting platform for the Queen's use and to take the salute. HMS *Surprise* was sold on 29 June 1965 and broken up at McLellan's, Bowness.

In 2006, for her eightieth birthday, and in July 2010, the Queen chartered the 2,112-gross-ton cruise ship *Hebridean Princess* for a ten-day private holiday voyage among the Western Isles ending by visiting the Castle of Mey Caithness. *Hebridean Princess*, built in 1964, began as the Caledonian-MacBrayne, 72-metre car ferry *Columba* on the Oban–Craignure–Lochaline service. In 1988, *Columba* was acquired when Hebridean Island Cruises was established and renamed *Hebridean Princess*, following a complete refit in 1989. This company failed and in April 2009 *Hebridean Princess* was bought by the UK-based All Leisure Group involved in cruise voyages worldwide.

Princess Elizabeth's day cabin aboard the royal tour ship *Gothic*. Mrs Audrey Cable, from Nelson, New Zealand, is busy arranging flowers on the writing desk Princess Elizabeth would use. The Princess' day room, with enormous windows, resembles the drawing room of an elegant English home. (J & C McCutcheon Collection)

Preparing the *Gothic* for the Royal Australian Tour at Southampton on 28 December 1951. The funnel of the liner has been extended by 6 feet so that the royal couple, Princess Elizabeth and the Duke of Edinburgh, would not be 'smoked off' the saluting platform, which had been built on top of the wheelhouse. (J & C McCutcheon Collection)

The royal tour ship is ready. A view of the anteroom aboard SS *Gothic*. Stewardess Miss R. Macinnon from the Isle of Skye is seen in the room. Much of the furniture seen here had come from the *Victoria and Albert* (III). (J & C McCutcheon Collection)

Departure day for the Royal Yacht *Gothic*, 10 November 1953, which would sail on to Jamaica and embark the royal party on 27 November. (J & C McCutcheon Collection)

An aerial view of part of the Coronation Naval Review, Spithead, 1953. The Trinity House *Patricia* is leading the Royal Yacht HMS *Surprise*. (Issued as a postcard by the defunct Raphael Tuck & Sons Ltd. Photographer unknown)

Royal barge from HMS *Jutland*. (J & C McCutcheon Collection)

HMS *Surprise* with HM The Queen on board at a Coronation Review, 19 June 1953.
(J & C McCutcheon Collection)

ROYAL YACHTS OF EUROPE

AUSTRIA-HUNGARY

The 330-ton, iron-hulled, paddle-yacht *Fantasie* was the first Imperial Yacht of Emperor Francis Joseph of the Austria-Hungary Empire. It was built in 1857 by Samuda Brothers at their shipyard at Poplar, London. It was two-masted, two-funnelled, and had a length of 176 feet, a beam of 16 feet, and a draught of 9 feet. In addition, it had oscillating steam engines producing 400 horsepower, giving a speed of 13 knots. It was used by the Emperor for private and State occasions on the Danube and occasionally in the Adriatic region. It was almost certainly the Imperial Austrian Yacht that conveyed Emperor Francis Joseph to the opening of the Suez Canal in 1869.

In 1872, *Fantasie* was replaced by the 1,830-ton, iron-hulled, paddle-yacht *Miramar*, also built by Samuda Brothers at Poplar, London. It was three-masted, two-funnelled, and had a length of 269 feet, a beam of 32 feet 8 inches, and a draught of 14 feet. Its direct-acting steam engines produced 2,500 indicated horsepower, giving a speed of 17 knots. It also had two fourteen-pounder guns and could, if needed, be pressed into service as a gunboat to support the Imperial Austro-Hungary Navy. Another example of this period was the 1,370-ton *Greif*, built 1885 at a shipyard in Pola (Pula), Croatia. It was transferred to Italy with the *Miramar* as war reparations in 1920. Emperor Francis Joseph's beautiful but unhappy wife, Empress Elizabeth, reputedly used to escape from the horrors (to her) of the Viennese Court in the *Greif* and *Miramar*, wandering all around the Mediterranean in them.

Several of the Habsburg family, who were part of the Austria-Hungary Empire, in addition to Emperor Francis Joseph, were enthusiastic personal yacht owners. An example was Archduke Carlo Stefano, a friend of Edward VII. One of his yachts was the steam-powered *Rovenska* that later in its career was to be used in experiments that changed the world's means of communication. The *Rovenska* was built for him by Ramage & Ferguson of Leith, Scotland, in 1904. Its name originated from an estate the Habsburgs owned on the island of Lussino. The *Rovenska* made several long cruises to St Petersburg, Russia, and also to various ports in Spain, due to the archduke being the brother of Maria Christina, Queen Mother of Spain and widow of King Alfonso XII. In 1909, *Rovenska* was sold to a Sir Max Waechter of London, who, in turn, sold it in 1914 to a Mr Gustavus M. E. Pratt, also of London. In the First World War, it was requisitioned as a Royal Navy patrol ship, and in February 1919 sold to Guglielmo Marconi, the wireless

The Imperial Austria-Hungary Archducal Yacht *Rovenska*, later owned by Marconi, renamed *Elettra* and used for wireless communication experiments. (Courtesy of Tomaso Gropallo, Genoa, Italy. Author's Collection)

communications pioneer, who renamed it *Elettra* and installed equipment for his experiments.

In June 1899, the French Government had placed a warship, *Ibis*, and storeship, *Vienne*, at Marconi's disposal, which he used steaming up and down the English Channel to hold successful test communications with South Foreland lighthouse, where he also had installed equipment. In September 1925, Marconi again used South Foreland lighthouse for experimental transmissions of a radio guidance system, where an aerial revolved every two minutes and sent code signals. The *Elettra* cruised the Goodwin Sands area off the Kent coast for seven hours, while British government and shipping experts on board saw this system successfully give all ships within a hundred miles a letter to indicate the ship's position, especially useful, it was claimed, in poor visibility.

On Marconi's death in 1937 *Elettra* was bought by the Italian government. During the Second World War, it was laid up in Trieste until taken over by the Kriegsmarine and refitted for use as an armed patrol ship. However, it was bombed and sunk near Zara, Yugoslavia. After the war the Yugoslav government raised it from the seabed and handed it to the Italian government. In 1962, it was in a derelict condition, comprising mainly its hull, in a dry dock at Muggia. After 1962, it was broken up, but parts were kept and given to relevant sites. The bow section is currently exhibited alongside a statue of Marconi near his mausoleum in the grounds of the Villa Grifone in Sassa Marconi, Bologna. The Villa Grifone was Marconi's birthplace and where he started his experiments in wireless telegraphy. It is now an Italian Government-owned museum housing some of his early experiments. A second part of the *Elettra* is on display at the Italian Telespazio Space Station and Marconi's wireless room from *Elettra* is exhibited at The Post Office Museum, Rome.

Another of Archduke Carlo Stefano's yachts was the 709-ton, steel-hulled *U1*. The name means 'hive', as in beehive, and Carlo reputedly named it this, when built for him in 1911 by Ramage & Ferguson, Leith, because if all his family were on board at the same time, it was as busy as a beehive. It was two-masted, single-funnelled, and had a length of 186 feet, a beam of 29 feet and a draught of 16 feet. In addition, the yacht had triple-expansion, three-cylinder steam engines fed by two boilers producing 138 horsepower. In the First World War, it was seized by Italian forces at Trieste, but when the King of Spain interceded, it was returned undamaged to Archduke Carlos. He sold it at the end of the war to A. J. Drexel, an American millionaire, who renamed it *Sayonara*.

BELGIUM

The 1,322-ton, steel-hulled, twin-screw schooner *Alberta* had the curious distinction of being a royal yacht that was not used by the monarch for official royal duties but only for commercial and other duties. It was built in 1896 by Ailsa Shipbuilding & Engineering Company, Troon, Scotland. It was two-masted, single-funnelled, and it had a length of 252 feet 6 inches, a beam of 33 feet 6 inches, and a draught of 15 feet 4 inches. In addition, it had two quadruple expansion, eight-cylinder steam engines built by D. Rowan & Son of Glasgow, fed by two boilers, producing 448 horsepower giving a speed of 17 knots. It was originally built as the *Margarita* for A. J. Drexel, the American millionaire who had bought *U1* from Archduke Carlos Stefano of Austria-Hungary. The King of the Belgians, Leopold II, bought it from Drexel in about 1899, renaming it *Alberta* and registering it under his agent's name, Little & Johnson. He also had a special harbour built for it at Cap Ferrat, France, where it was frequently moored while he lived aboard and used it as an office for the commercial ventures that made him personally wealthy. On finishing work every day, he left the ship and on the quay climbed onto a motor-tricycle and drove off to the Villa des Cedres to spend time with his mistress, Caroline Lacroix. Leopold died in 1909, after which the *Alberta* served as the renamed *Rozsviet* in the Russian Navy.

The SS *Titanic* at Cowes, 10 April 1912. To the left can be seen the Belgian Royal Yacht *Alberta*. (J & C McCutcheon Collection)

BULGARIA

The 715-ton, steel-hulled *Nadiejda*, with a ram-like bow, was built in 1898 at Bordeaux, France, as a torpedo gunboat. It was two-masted, single-funnelled, and had a length of 200 feet, a beam of 23 feet and a draught of 12 feet. It also had two sets of triple-expansion steam engines fed by French water-tube boilers giving a speed of 17 knots. It was converted at an unknown date to be the Bulgarian royal yacht, with the addition of more accommodation and an aft deckhouse, almost certainly being used on the River Danube, the Black Sea and Mediterranean for French and other area port visits. It ceased to be the royal yacht for King Boris of Bulgaria in 1943.

DENMARK

The 740-ton, paddle-schooner *Slesvig* was built in 1845 by Robert Napier of Glasgow, as *Copenhagen*. It was three-masted, single-funnelled, and had a length of 54 metres, a beam of 7.85 metres, and a draught of 2.5 metres. It also had side-lever-type steam engines producing 240 horsepower, giving a speed of 10 knots. As *Copenhagen* it was used between Kiel and Copenhagen as a packet boat, but it was taken over by the Danish Navy in 1848, renamed *Slesvig*, and used for numerous purposes, such as a troop transport and mail boat. King Christian IX agreed to it being converted to a royal yacht for him in 1856, and he sailed on it until 1879, apart from 1864 when it was fitted with twelve three-pounder guns and used as a tender to the *Dannebrog* during the Schleswig-Holstein War. In 1879, its use as a royal yacht ended, it being superceded by *Dannebrog* (I), and it was broken up in 1894.

In 1879, the 770-ton, steel-hulled, paddle-schooner *Dannebrog* (I) was built by Burmeister & Wain, Copenhagen, for King Christian IX, being launched on 6 October. It was two-masted, two-funnelled, and had a length of 199 feet, a beam of 26 feet 8 inches, and a draught of 10 feet 4 inches. In addition, it was fitted with compound, four-cylinder steam engines providing 376 horsepower. It had no figurehead but on each of the paddle boxes were mounted the Danish national coat of arms. These are now preserved in Orlogsmuseet, Copenhagen, since the *Dannebrog* (I) was scrapped at Copenhagen in June 1934. King Christian IX was a member of the British Royal Yacht Squadron and he and *Dannebrog* (I) regularly attended Cowes Week.

The ship was in service from 1879 until 1931, when the 1,070-ton, steel-hulled, twin-screw schooner *Dannebrog* (II) was built by the Royal Dockyard, Copenhagen, for King Christian X. It is two-masted, single-funnelled, with a clipper-ship hull style and it has a length of 207 feet, a beam of 34 feet, and a draught of 11 feet 6 inches. It also has two four-cylinder diesel engines built by Burmeister and Wain. After the Second World War, *Dannebrog* (II) was used by King Frederick IX, and more recently Queen Margarethe, for private and State visits. Other Danish royal yachts were the seventeenth-century *Elephanten* and the *Birma*.

FRANCE

The first Imperial French Yacht was the three-masted, single-funnelled, paddle-schooner *L'Aigle*, built in France in 1858, with a length of 160 feet, a beam of

25 feet and a draught of 10 feet. It had simple oscillating steam engines driving the paddle wheels. As was the fashion at the time, it had a figurehead of a gold-painted eagle, the black hull being relieved by a row of imitation gun-ports that in reality were white-shuttered portholes. Emperor Napoleon III used *L'Aigle* extensively in the Mediterranean and North Sea and, being a member of the British Royal Yacht Squadron, attending Cowes Week regatta. For one of its most notable tasks, however, Napoleon III was not aboard, being busy with affairs of state, so his wife, Empress Eugenie, sailed on it to attend the opening of the newly finished Suez Canal on 16 November 1869. As the canal was the achievement of a Frenchman, Ferdinand de Lesseps, who was Eugenie's cousin, it was appropriate that, on 18 November, *L'Aigle*, with Empress Eugenie on board, led royal yachts *Mahroussa* and *Fantasie*, from Egypt and Austria-Hungary respectively, ahead of a flotilla of other craft through the canal to declare it open for use.

The next Imperial French Yacht, the three-masted, one-funnelled, iron-hulled, screw-barquentine *Jerome Napoleon,* was an amalgam of sail and steam, with very substantial masts and sails to aid the engines. It was built in France in 1859 and had a length of 230 feet, a beam of 24 feet and a draught of 12 feet. In addition, it had early two-stage-expansion steam engines fed by fire-tube boilers, driving a large, single screw. It was named after Napoleon III's cousin, Prince Jerome Napoleon, and used by the Imperial French Royal Family and the French Navy until about 1867, when it was replaced by the three-masted, one-funnelled *La Reine Hortense.* This vessel was built by Normand Shipyard at Le Havre as *Patriote,* then renamed *Comte d'Eu* and *Cassard* until acquired in 1867 as the royal yacht and named *La Reine Hortense.* It was of similar size and had the same engines as its predecessor, *Jerome Napoleon,* together with substantial masts and sails. *La Reine Hortense* was the last Imperial French royal yacht.

GERMANY

The iron-hulled, paddle-schooner *Kaiseradler* was built at Kiel, Germany, by the Germania Werst shipyard in 1875. It was two-masted, two-funnelled, the funnels having bell-mouth tops and it had a length of 268 feet, a beam of 34 feet and a draught of 14 feet. In addition, it was fitted with oscillating two-cylinder steam engines with fire-tube boilers, producing 3,000 indicated horsepower giving a speed of 15 knots. It is probable Kaiser Wilhelm II, who became ruler of Germany in 1888, used *Kaiseradler* while taking part in regattas held in the Baltic. The Imperial German Yacht *Grille* was another used for these by the Kaiser. Little is recorded of its condition and background except that it was built approximately in the 1880s in Germany, and that it was a wooden-hulled, three-masted, one-funnelled screw-schooner, with a length of 160 feet, a beam of 19 feet 5 inches and a draught of 9 feet, possibly having two compound steam engines driving twin screws.

The ship, when it arrived at Cowes to attend the Cowes Week Regatta, was the pride and joy of Kaiser Wilhelm II, a member of the British Royal Yacht Squadron. However, what aroused the chagrin of Edward VII when Prince of Wales and others was the Kaiser's 4,280-ton, steel-hulled, twin-screw schooner *Hohenzollern,* with a ram bow bearing a figurehead of a German Imperial double-eagle crest. It was built at Stettin in 1892 by the Vulcan Shipbuilding Company to a German Admiralty design and was launched on 27 June 1892. It was three-masted, two-funnelled, also with the funnels having bell-mouth funnel tops, and it had a length of 382 feet 6 inches, a beam of 45 feet 9 inches, and a draught of

23 feet. In addition, it had two triple-expansion steam engines fed by eight boilers, producing 9,600 indicated horsepower giving a speed of 21.5 knots, the engines also being made by Vulcan, Stettin.

On 20 June 1895, *Hohenzollern* steamed through the Holtenan Locks to declare the Kaiser Wilhelm Canal (later renamed simply the Kiel Canal) officially open. The ship was much used on Baltic, North Sea and Mediterranean coasts for courtesy and prestige visits.

In 1902, the Kaiser's first racing schooner, *Meteor* (III), designed by Cary Smith, an American, was built in the USA and *Hohenzollern*, with Prince Henry of Prussia on board, attended the launching there. However, by 1892, *Hohenzollern* was soon smaller than the royal yachts of several other nations, so Kaiser Wilhelm implemented the building of a larger, luxurious 7,300-ton replacement, 520 feet in length with a clipper, not ram, bow and a clipper stern. Work began on it in 1914 at Vulcan Shipbuilding Company's shipyard, but the start of the First World War stopped labouring work on this new example, which was not commenced again at the end of the war and in 1923 *Hohenzollern* (II) was broken up.

In his attempt to supercede Edward VII and then George V as the supreme of yachtsmen at Cowes and elsewhere, Kaiser Wilhelm II owned a succession of large racing yachts from the first, a cutter named *Thistle* and renamed *Meteor* (I), to a schooner, *Meteor* (V). One of the most successful was the 400-ton, steel-hulled, gaff topsail, two-masted schooner *Meteor* (IV), built at Kiel by Germania Werst in 1909. It had a length of 129 feet 2 inches, a beam of 27 feet 15 inches and a draught of 14 feet 8 inches. Like the earlier examples, it took part in Kiel Regatta Week as a member of the Imperial Yacht Club, of which Kaiser Wilhelm was patron, but it was the more prestigious Cowes Week Regatta where he and other yacht owners wanted to succeed and be seen to do so.

The German Imperial Yacht *Hohenzollern* as between the years 1893 and 1906. (Courtesy of the Deutsche Museum, Munich. Author's Collection)

Hohenzollern on the Kaiser Wilhelm Canal.

Kaiser's Yacht *Hohenzollern*. (J & C McCutcheon Collection)

German Royal Yacht *Hohenzollern*. (J & C McCutcheon Collection)

The Emperor of Germany's Royal Yacht *Hohenzollern*, Portsmouth, November 1907.

The German Emperor's Yacht *Hohenzollern*.

Hohenzollern.

The *Thistle*, yacht of HM The Empress Eugenie. (See page 126.) (J & C McCutcheon Collection)

Führer Adolf Hitler, Dictator Chancellor of the German Reich, also 'possessed' an 85-foot-long yacht, *Ostwind*, which is German for 'east wind'. Following Hitler's anger at the poor yachting display of the German entrants in the 1936 Olympic Games, he ordered the building of a series of racing yachts to improve performances of future entrants; *Ostwind* was built at Bremen in 1939. He is known to have visited *Ostwind* several times, occasionally with Eva Braun, but it is not known if he actually sailed on it. The *Ostwind* was captured by the United States Navy at the end of the Second World War, and then passed through several hands, including a group hoping to convert it into a museum. This came to nothing and *Ostwind* ended up in a Jacksonville shipyard, Florida, for seven years. Knowing its background, it was then badly vandalised. The American Nazi Party tried to buy it, but was refused. The Israeli Consulate in the USA, hearing of this, suggested to the Miami Beach Commissioner that *Ostwind* be sunk somewhere suitable to create a reef as a sanctuary for marine life. In June 1989, this was done off Miami Beach, achieved in a few minutes by tipping it off a barge, the derelict *Ostwind* rapidly disappearing beneath the surface forever.

GREECE

The Greek Royal Family used a steam yacht, *Spaktena* (or *Sfakteria*?), as their royal yacht. In 1917, King Constantine I and the Royal Family sailed on *Spaktena* when leaving Greece for Italy en route to exile in Switzerland. The country had a habit of deposing and reinstating its monarchs. King George II, who had been deposed in 1924, returned as king in 1933 and is believed to have used *Spaktena* again for family and State purposes. He did attend Cowes Week on this royal yacht as a member of the British Royal Yacht Squadron. The Greek Royal Family had and has a reputation for their skill with racing yachts, such as the Dragon Class; Prince Constantine, later king, won an Olympic gold medal for Greece in 1960.

ITALY

The 2,850-ton, three-masted, one-funnelled, screw-barquentine *Savoia* (I), named after the Italian Royal House of Savoy, with a clipper ship bow, built at Castellammare di Stabia in 1883, was the first Italian royal yacht. It had a length of 304 feet 9 inches, a beam of 41 feet 4 inches, and had three-cylinder horizontal steam engines, built by Penn, fed by eight boilers producing 3,340 horsepower, which gave a speed of 15 knots. King Umberto I owned it in 1900 and it was frequently used by him for family and State occasions in the Adriatic and Mediterranean regions, but it was disposed of in 1902, becoming, after a refit, the naval floating workshop *Vulcan* until 1923.

The 9,199-ton Italian royal yacht *Trinacria*, which followed the *Savoia* (I), was another example of a ship that started its seagoing career as something different and went through other purposes until its final duty. It began as the 5,528-ton, steel-hulled *America*, which was two-masted, with two tall, elliptical funnels and a clipper bow. It was built in 1883 for the British National Steamship Company by J. & G. Thomson shipyard, Glasgow. It had a length of 462 feet 8 inches and a beam of 50 feet 6 inches. It was powered by Thomson three-cylinder, double-expansion steam engines fed by six boilers, producing 6,120 horsepower and giving a speed of 15 knots. Appropriately, its figurehead was a crowned female figure, 'America', flanked on each side by the Stars and Stripes shield of the United States. The National Steamship Company's intention was to use it to win the Blue Riband for the fastest Atlantic crossing. On its maiden voyage in May 1884, it achieved an outward record of six days, fifteen hours and twenty-two minutes from Queenstown to New York, and an average speed of 17.8 knots homeward, but in two months that record was beaten. It continued an express service between Liverpool and New York, but in 1887 the daily coal consumption of 190 tons made it uneconomic to run; the National Steamship Company sold it to the Italian government for use in the Italian Navy. The latter retained its name *America* for several years, using it as the flagship cruiser of the Italian Expeditionary Force to Eritrea in 1887. After use as a cruiser, it was a transport, and a ship used as a torpedo school. In November 1891, by government order, it was renamed *Trinacria* and lavishly refitted in 1900 to become the Italian royal yacht. On the ship Crown Prince Vittorio Emmanuelle of Italy and his bride, Princess Elena of Montenegro, spent their lengthy honeymoon cruising the Mediterranean and sailed to Scandinavia. During 1921–22, *Trinacria* was used as an exhibition ship, then scrapped in 1925 and replaced as a royal yacht by the 5,365-ton, two-masted, two-funnelled, steel-hulled, twin-screw schooner *Savoia* (II), which was built at the Royal Italian Arsenal, La Spezia, in 1923, as the *Cita di Palermo*. It had a length of 390 feet, a beam of 49 feet 2 inches, and a draught of 15 feet. It was powered by a single Parsons steam turbine engine geared to two shafts fed by eight Yarrow boilers producing 12,000 horsepower giving a speed of 21 knots. In 1925, at Palermo, Sicily, *Cita di Palermo* was converted by Cantieri Navali Riuniti to be the royal yacht and renamed *Savoia* (II) for extensive use by King Victor Emmanuelle III. Early during the Second World War, it was laid up at Ancona, Italy, but at the Italian Armistice was captured by German forces and converted to an armed patrol ship. During an Allied air raid on Ancona in 1944, *Savoia* (II), lying off the port, was bombed and sunk, its wreck being found on the Adriatic Sea bed after the war.

Another example of an Italian royal yacht was the 252-gross-ton, steel-hulled, two-masted, one-funnelled *Jela*, built at Glasgow in 1891. It was privately owned by Prince Vittorio Emanuele III, and he was on board on 29 July 1900 when he

The Italian Royal Yacht *Savoia* (I), built in 1883, and owned in 1900 by King Umberto I of Italy. (Courtesy of the La Spezia Naval Museum, Italy. Author's collection)

The Italian Royal Yacht *Trinacria*. (Courtesy of La Spezia Naval Museum, Italy. Author's collection)

The Italian Royal Yacht *Jela*, owned by Prince Vittorio Emanuele III, later King of Italy, built in 1891. (Courtesy of La Spezia Naval Museum. Author's collection)

learned that his father, King Umberto I, had been murdered and he was thus king. In 1915, *Jela* sailed under the colours of the Royal Italian Yacht Club, its fate being unknown.

Benito Mussolini, Il Duce, Dictator of Italy, also used a small, armed yacht on several occasions. Built in England in 1905 for a private owner, it was sold to the Imperial Austro-Hungarian Navy and named *Taurus*, being used as a guardship at the Austrian Embassy, Constantinople, Turkey. In 1918, it was transferred as war reparation to the Royal Italian Navy and renamed *Marechiaro*. Converted to a 950-ton armed yacht, it had two rapid-firing 57-mm guns. In 1925, it was refitted at Moggiano, La Spezia, as a luxurious yacht for Mussolini and renamed *Aurora*. Like Mussolini, its luck ran out, and in 1943, after the Italian Armistice it sailed from Zara for Ancona on 11 September, but off Ancona was attacked and sunk by two torpedoes from a German warship.

MONACO

The early royal yachts of this principality were used for a special, scientific purpose – oceanographic research. In 1873, after finishing training service in the Spanish Navy and wartime service in the French Navy, Prince Albert I of Monaco, great-grandfather of the late Prince Rainier III, visited England and while at Torquay bought the 200-ton sailing schooner then named *Pleiad*. He renamed it *Hirondelle* (I) and sailed it back to Monaco. In this vessel he carried out his preliminary training in oceanography. In July 1885, *Hirondelle* (I), with Prince Albert and a crew of fifteen, most of them Scots or Bretons, sailed from the Breton port of Lorient for a two-month survey expedition, mostly pelagic fishing (deep sea) in the Bay of Biscay and the eastern Atlantic to the Azores. For many years all the sounding and dredging on *Hirondelle* (I) was done by hand; the hand-operated winches required six of the crew for each winch and it took on average nine hours to haul up a dredge from a depth of 2,800 metres. This royal yacht is commemorated by the Hirondelle Deep, a channel between the islands of Terceira, St Michael's and Ponta Delgada, Azores, its depth of 1,900 fathoms sounded for the first time by Prince Albert.

Further research was postponed for three years after Prince Albert succeeded to the throne of Monaco in 1889, but in 1892, he turned again to oceanographic research. He had ordered the 600-ton, single-screw, three-masted, single-stove-pipe-funnelled, auxiliary-topsail schooner *Princess Alice* (I) built by Green & Co., London, which was completed in 1891. It had a length of 180 feet, a beam of 27 feet and a draught of 12 feet. It was powered by simple-expansion, three-cylinder steam engines, by Penn & Co., producing 64 horsepower. It was specially fitted out for this type of research with steam-powered equipment and with several well-equipped laboratories on the main deck. From 1892 to 1897, *Princess Alice* (I) was used in research and surveys in the Mediterranean and North Atlantic. The first voyage in 1892 was to the western Mediterranean, where research observations took place into temperatures and densities of sea water. The name of the ship was given to an extensive shoal south-west of Fayal Island, Azores, the Princess Alice Bank discovered during one of the surveys in the area.

Following this, Prince Albert I ordered an even more powerful royal yacht, the 1,378-gross-ton *Princess Alice* (II). It was a steel-hulled, two-masted, one-funnelled auxiliary schooner, built by Laird & Co., Birkenhead, in 1897. It had a length of 245 feet, a beam of 35 feet, a draught of 9 feet 7 inches, and two boilers and engines that produced 116 horsepower. It also had sails made by Ratsey & Lapthorn. Its steam-operated winches, with 12,000 metres of cable, made it possible to take soundings at very considerable depths. From 1898 to 1910, it was used on expeditions to the Arctic north of Spitzbergen and also in the north Atlantic and Mediterranean in 1906–07. In 1902, it became world famous while on a Mediterranean survey for saving the life of the Brazilian aviator Santos Dumont, who, on 14 February, was carrying out an experiment with his airship *Santos Dumont 6* when it apparently flew into an air pocket. This had the effect of violently pitching the airship, which lost its rudder and engine and collapsed into the sea. As the airship's basket sank, Dumont was up to his neck in the water when rescued. The *Princess Alice* (II) then towed the wreck of the airship back to Monaco.

In 1906, Prince Albert I founded the Museum of Oceanography, Monaco, to fulfil his dream inspired by his expeditionary voyages. It was on board *Princess Alice* (II), with marine scientists from the Museum of Oceanography, that he and they discovered anaphylaxie, the poison used by jellyfish to paralyse fish and small marine life. This poison, when extracted, had bacteriological and pathological uses. The final royal yacht that Prince Albert I used in this manner was *Hirondelle* (II), built by Forges and Chantiers de la Méditerranée Société Anonyme, Le Havre, at their La Seyne shipyard in 1911. The steel-hulled, 1,771-gross-ton *Hirondelle* (II) had a length of 291 feet 6 inches, a beam of 36 feet and a depth of 17 feet 6 inches. It also had four boilers, the engines producing 236 horsepower. It was equipped with the most up-to-date scientific equipment of the time in its laboratories. Most of its research surveys were carried out in the Mediterranean and North Atlantic from 1911 to 1915. Prince Albert I died in June 1922.

There were other royal yachts of Monaco. Notable was the 133-foot-long *Deo Juvante* (II), built by Camper & Nicholson, Southampton, in 1928, equipped with

The *Princess Alice* (II), the oceanography Royal Yacht of Prince Albert I, lying off Monaco. (Courtesy of H. Murphy, Brixham)

two Gardner engines giving it a cruising speed of 11 knots. Prince Rainier III met his future wife, actress Grace Kelly, on *Deo Juvante* (II) on her arrival off Monte Carlo in the US liner *Constitution* on 12 April 1956. After their wedding they sailed on the *Deo Juvante* (II) for Villefranche, Valencia and Majorca. It was sold in 1957 and replaced by the three-masted *Costa del Sol* that had an oceanography purpose. Formerly a Mediterranean cargo ship plying between Malaga and Marseilles, it was stripped down to its wooden hull, fitted with a lounge saloon, staterooms and four bathrooms. The hull was painted white. In the aft of the ship was a marine laboratory with tanks for preserving fish specimens. It was sold to an Italian soft-drinks manufacturer in 1961.

The *Albercaro* (II) was built in Holland in 1963 at a cost of £250,000, named after Prince Albert and Princess Caroline, two of the royal children. On its final trials before being handed over there was a serious fire that badly damaged the engine room, so it was not handed over to its owner until March 1964. In December 1964, it was sold to Sheikh Shakbut, Ruler of Abu Dhabi. It was sailed from Monaco to Abu Dhabi and undertook one voyage in the Persian Gulf. However, afterwards it was moored unused at Abu Dhabi's jetty.

Also named after the royal children Princess Caroline, Princess Stephanie and Prince Albert was the Monegasque motor cruiser *Carostefal*, bought in 1964. Prince Rainier's motor yacht in 1975 was the 80-ton *Stalca*, also named using parts of his children's names. Another Monegasque royal yacht was the *Cecelia*.

The *Costa del Sol*, formerly a cargo ship until converted to a royal yacht. (Courtesy of the late Prince Rainier III of Monaco. Author's collection)

The *Albercaro* (II), named after the royal children of Prince Albert and Princess Caroline, the name being below the bridge. (Courtesy of the late Prince Rainier III of Monaco. Author's collection)

The motor cruiser *Carostefal* in front of the Museum of Oceanography, Monaco, which was founded by Prince Albert I. (Courtesy of the late Prince Rainier III of Monaco. Author's collection)

The *Cecelia*, a royal yacht used by Prince Rainier III and the Monegasque Royal Family. (Courtesy of the late Prince Rainier III of Monaco. Author's collection)

NETHERLANDS

The first Dutch royal yacht was the 810-ton, wooden-hulled, single-masted, one-funnelled paddle-steamer *De Leeuw* (*The Lion*), built at the Navy Yard, Rotterdam, in 1826–27. It had a length of 37 metres, a beam of 5.7 metres, a draught of 2 metres, and a simple, diagonal-compound engine producing 50 horsepower to drive the paddle wheels; their boxes had a mass of ornate decoration, including the Royal Dutch coat-of-arms and the bows had a lion figurehead. It was launched in 1827 and was much used by King William II and his family on official and private occasions, such as for the Review of the Dutch Naval Fleet at Flushing Roads in June 1843. In 1882, *De Leeuw* was withdrawn from royal service to be used as a training ship for engineers at Hellevoetsluis instead, until broken up in 1893.

It was replaced by the *Valk* in 1882. This 1,218-TM- (Thames Measurement) ton, two-masted, two-funnelled, wooden-hulled, paddle-wheel schooner was built 1863–64 at the Navy Yard, Amsterdam. It had a length of 250 feet, a beam of 31 feet and a draught of 12 feet. Its oscillating two-cylinder steam engines driving the paddle wheels and produced a speed of 12 knots. It was much used for regional visits by King William III, who was also a member of the British Royal Yacht Squadron and came to Cowes Week on *Valk*, also bringing members of the Dutch Royal Family to Britain for informal visits in 1882, 1884 and 1895. One of these visits included Princess Wilhelmina, who became Queen in 1890. By 1898, *Valk* was obsolete and broken up in 1899.

More recent is the 151-TM-tons, twin-screw motor-yacht *Piet Hein*, named after a famous Dutch Admiral. Built by N. V. Amsterdamsiber Scheeps in Amsterdam in 1937, as a wedding present for the then Princess (later Queen) Juliana and Prince Bernhard. It was steel-hulled, with a length of 101 feet 7 inches, a beam of 18 feet 7 inches and a draught of 5 feet. The two DAF, six-cylinder diesel engines produced 100 horsepower. It was used for personal and State purposes on Netherlands inland waterways.

NORWAY

The Norwegian government of 1905, after the dissolution of the union with Sweden, formally invited Prince Carl of Denmark to become King of Norway. Among the proposals put to him was that he would be provided with a royal yacht financed by the Norwegian government. Prince Carl accepted the invitation to become King Haakon of Norway, but on doing so, due to the economic situation of Norway at the time, did not enforce the supply of a royal yacht. During the interwar years, this proposal was in abeyance until after the Second World War, when it was brought up in part by Norwegian newspapers, who published an appeal to the Norwegian people to donate required funds to present King Haakon with such a yacht on his seventy-fifth birthday. The Norwegians donated large and small sums towards the cost of its purchase and those who did so were proud to know they had contributed towards the gift so the nation had a royal yacht. Would the British people be less charitable if there was a similar opportunity for Britain to have a new royal yacht?

The 1,611-ton Norwegian Royal Yacht *Norge* began as the diesel yacht *Philante*, built by Camper & Nicholson at Southampton in 1937 for British aircraft manufacturer and industrialist Thomas O. M. Sopwith. He used it as a base when competing in regattas and in his ownership, in 1938, took part in a

The Dutch nineteenth-century paddle-wheel Royal Yacht *De Leeuw*. Note the Dutch Royal Coat of Arms on the paddle box and ornate decoration on the stern. (Ned. Hist. Scheepvaart, Amsterdam)

The Dutch nineteenth-century paddle-wheel Royal Yacht *Valk* under way behind a paddle-wheel tug. Place and event unknown. Some of the crowd have an L. S. Lowry appearance. Judging by the large number of people, this is an important occasion, but not important enough for the man on the trestle, bottom right, who turned to look at the photographer. (Ned. Hist. Scheepvaart Museum, Amsterdam)

The *Philante*, which later became the Norwegian Royal Yacht *Norge*. (J & C McCutcheon Collection)

regatta at Hanko in eastern Norway. The name was an amalgam of Sopwith's wife's Christian name, Phyllis, and his name, Thomas: 'Phil' short for Phyllis plus 'an' short for and, plus 't' for Thomas, and 'e' to add an extra syllable.

The ship was two-masted, one-funnelled, steel-hulled, with a length of 263 feet, a beam of 38 feet, and a draught 14 feet 5 inches. It was powered by two MAN, eight-cylinder diesel engines producing 3,000 horsepower providing a speed of 14 knots. It was requisitioned from Sopwith by the Royal Navy for sea service in the Second World War, as an escort vessel for Atlantic convoys, then in 1942 as a school ship for training convoy escorts. In 1946, the Royal Navy returned *Philante* to Sopwith. In July 1947, he accepted an offer for it of NOK 1.5 million from the Association of Norwegian Ship Owners, whereon it was refitted as the Royal Norwegian Yacht and renamed *Norge*. In fact, *Norge* was being refurbished at the time so King Haakon, a member of the British Royal Yacht Squadron, was given a model of the ship on his seventy-fifth birthday.

On 17 May 1948, the captain of *Norge*, Commander Christian Monsen, raised the command pennant for the first time and on 9 June the full size *Norge* was presented to King Haakon. He substantially used it to visit the coastal communities of Norway and to voyage abroad. In June 1955, a visit to Molde, West Norway, was to be his last voyage on the yacht and he passed away in 1957. His son, now King Olav, took over and continued to use the *Norge* in an official capacity as well as for leisure. In 1985, *Norge* was seriously damaged in a fire while in dry dock at Horten shipyard to be repaired and refitted, but King Olav decided to rebuild and restore it and this was done over the next year. After King Olav passed away in 1991, his son Harald, now king, took over *Norge* to use as a base when taking part in major yacht races and regattas. It was also used by King Harald and Queen Sonja for official engagements and State occasions in Norway and overseas. In 1991 and 1992, the couple used it to visit southern Norway and northern Norway respectively to celebrate their consecration. In the summer of 1997, King Harald and Queen Sonja invited members of the European royal families to join a celebration of their sixtieth birthdays, part of which was a cruise from Trondheim to Lofoten on board *Norge*, the royal yacht *Dannebrog* and a Norwegian Navy ship KNM *Horten*.

The sailing schedule for *Norge* varies annually, but basically the summer season is started when the King embarks for inspection, usually around mid-May, and is closed when he disembarks in late September. Maintenance of *Norge* is done by the crew during winter, being manned, operated and maintained by the Norwegian armed forces. In February, annually a group of new 'recruits' from the Norwegian Navy report to the ship for duty to start the theoretical and practical training for the coming year aboard.

PORTUGAL

King Carlos I, who became King of Portugal in 1889, was another European monarch who used his royal yachts for oceanographic research. He also named three of them *Amelia*, after his wife. In the first, the 150-ton *Amelia* (I), he did much marine research off the west coast of Portugal in 1896. The second example, the 300-ton *Amelia* (II), built by Ramage & Ferguson of Leith in 1880, was firstly named *Fair Geraldine*, then *Geraldine*. This three-masted, one-funnelled, iron-hulled, topsail-screw schooner had a length of 148 feet, a beam of 21 feet, and a draught of 11 feet, and was fitted with compound-steam, two-cylinder inverted engines producing 55 horsepower. In this royal yacht, King Carlos undertook oceanographic expeditions in 1897 and 1898. The third example, the 650-ton *Amelia* (III), firstly named *Banshee*, was built in 1900, also by Ramage & Ferguson, Leith, to a Cox & King design. This two-masted, two-funnelled, steel-hulled, twin-screw schooner with a ram bow had a length of 229 feet, a beam of 29 feet 6 inches, and a draught of 10 feet 6 inches. In addition, it was fitted with two triple-expansion, six-cylinder steam engines fed by two boilers producing 386 horsepower. When Colonel Harry MacCalmont, its original owner, died in 1904, the Portuguese government bought it as a royal yacht for King Carlos and it was renamed *Amelia* (III). In this yacht, off the Algarve coast of Portugal, King Carlos studied the migrations of tunny fish to and from the Mediterranean.

After the assassination of King Carlos and one of his sons in 1908, the last duty of *Amelia* (III) as a royal yacht was to sail to Gibraltar in 1910, taking the surviving Portuguese Royal Family into exile. In 1911, the Republic of Portugal converted *Amelia* (III) to an armed despatch ship and renamed it 5 *de Outubro*, but it was also used frequently as a survey ship for the Portuguese Navy. In 1936, its use was again changed to become an armed naval cruiser, its eventual fate being unknown. King Carlos also owned several other royal yachts at various times – the 635-ton *Yacoma*, and the 64-ton *Sado*, ex-*Banshee*, were two; also used by the Portuguese Royal Family and State were *Sirius*, *Lia* ex-*Mida*, *Madedja*, *Veloz*, *Nautilus* and *Aura*.

ROUMANIA

The *Luceafarul* was a royal yacht associated with two kings who abdicated. It was originally named *Nahlin*, having been ordered to design by Lady Yule in 1929 from G. L. Watson & Co. Her requirement was that it should allow her to 'visit every part of the globe she desired'. The 260-foot, two-masted, single-funnelled steam yacht with clipper bow and counter stern was built by John Brown & Co.,

The yacht *Nahlin*, which would later become the Roumanian Royal Yacht *Luceafarul*.

Govan. Its accommodation and furnishings were opulent in style. Lady Yule used it for some lengthy cruises, including one circumnavigation, and then offered it for charter to others so inclined. In the summer of 1936, it was chartered by King Edward VIII, and he and Mrs Wallis Simpson cruised the Adriatic and Aegean Seas to Istanbul, Turkey. Edward abdicated in December 1936 and married Mrs Simpson shortly afterwards. King Carol II of Roumania, like the rest of the world, noted the news of this romance and use of *Nahlin*. In 1937, it was bought by the Roumanian government for £120,000 to become the Roumanian Royal Yacht for King Carol, renaming it *Luceafarul*. He used it for a similar purpose for himself and his mistress, Madame Elena Lupescu, in July 1939, cruising on the Aegean Sea and to Crete. When King Carol abdicated in 1940, the second king associated with *Nahlin/Luceafarul* to do so, it became state-owned, was renamed *Libertatea*, spending much time moored at Constanza until converted to a floating restaurant and used for thirty years. In 1989, it was discovered by a British yacht broker, still being so used on a Roumanian backwater and in a sadly declined condition.

When the Roumanian Communist State collapsed, the ship was bought by a private local company, but in 1999, a British company purchased it from them and had it brought to England by heavy-lifter ship for it to be restored to its former splendour. Ironically, the company that designed it in 1929, G. L. Watson & Co., was involved through its archives with their sister company Yachtworks in stabilising the ship's interior and to restore it overall.

IMPERIAL TSARIST RUSSIA

The 11,802-TM-ton, steel-hulled *Livadia* was almost certainly the most incredible royal yacht ever built, definitely so in a British shipyard, due to it being elliptical in plan. It was built by John Elder & Co., Govan, Glasgow, in 1880, to a design based on Imperial Russian Admiralty plans, with a length of 266 feet, an enormous beam of 153 feet and a draught of 6 feet 5 inches. It had three sets of compound two-stage-expansion steam engines fed by eight in-line athwartships boilers, producing 10,500 indicated horsepower and giving a speed of 15.9 knots. Its turbot-like lower hull was the area for engines and boilers, and to supply the relevant buoyancy for its eccentric shape, plus it was also built with a double bottom divided into watertight compartments. The upper hull appeared more like a conventional ship, with accommodation for guests and crew, all done in considerable luxury, even down to a fountain encircled by beds of flowers and foliage. It might be thought that its shape would mean excessive rolling of the ship to the consternation of all aboard, but in crossing the shallow Black Sea this was not so. Ordered for Tsar Alexander II in 1880, by the time *Livadia* was built and arrived in Sebastopol, Tsar Alexander had been murdered and the Imperial Russian Family never sailed on it. It was replaced in 1888 by *Pole Star* and was laid up in a dry dock at Sebastopol finally being broken up in 1926. Fortunately, the dream of building a successful circular or even elliptical-shaped ship also died in due course.

The 3,270-TM-ton, steel-hulled, three-masted, two-funnelled, twin-screw schooner *Pole Star* (*Poliarnaia Zvesda*) was built by Baltiiski Shipbuilding Company, St Petersburg, in 1888, with a length of 336 feet 5 inches, a beam of 46 feet and a draught of 15 feet. It was powered by two Baltiiski six-cylinder, compound steam engines fed by ten boilers producing 7,496 horsepower. It was used for cruising the Baltic with Tsar Alexander III, his wife, Marie Fedorovna, and other members of the Imperial Russian Family and Court. During the cruise, a call was usually made to Sweden to visit the Swedish Royal Family and sometimes other royal yachts would attend to create a sort of Royal Yacht Family soirée. However, on 20 June 1894, *Pole Star* arrived at Gravesend with Tsarevitch Nicholas of Russia (later Nicholas II) on board and was met by Prince Louis of Battenberg. Nicholas stayed several days with Prince Louis and his wife, Princess Victoria of Hesse (granddaughter of Queen Victoria), and Tsarevitch Nicholas's fiancée, Princess Alexandra of Hesse (Princess Victoria's youngest sister and granddaughter of Queen Victoria), and to be 'overseen' by Queen Victoria. In October 1894, *Pole Star* conveyed the seriously ill Tsar Alexander III, father of Nicholas II, to Yalta, Crimea. From there he travelled to the Livadia Palace, the latter name used for the Imperial Russian yacht, where he died on 1 November 1894.

The Imperial Russian yacht used by Tsar Nicholas II and the Russian Royal Family was the 4,334-TM-ton, steel-hulled, three-masted, two-funnelled, twin-screw schooner *Standart*, built by Burmeister & Wain, Copenhagen, in 1895. It had a length of 420 feet, a beam of 50 feet 4 inches, and a draught of 20 feet, and was powered by two Burmeister & Wain triple-expansion, six-cylinder steam engines fed by twenty-four boilers, providing 10,600 indicated horsepower and a speed of 18 knots. The *Standart* was used for family and State ceremonial occasions, including attendance at Cowes Regatta. In the summer of 1908, Tsar Nicholas II, with his wife, Alexandra, now Empress Alexandra, with the Dowager Empress Marie, sister of Queen Alexandra, wife of Edward VII, sailed in the *Standart* from St Petersburg to Tallinn (then Revel) to meet Edward and Queen Alexandra on *Victoria and Albert* (III), which was anchored near the other Imperial Russian Yacht, *Pole Star*. This was the occasion when the women choristers in a choral society due to perform a concert for the illustrious guests, were stripped and searched by Russian security men before the concert was allowed to start, such was the fear of assassination of Russian royalty at that time. In June 1914, Tsar Nicholas II and Empress Alexandra undertook a cruise in *Standart* on the Black Sea, visiting Constanza, Roumania, and calling on the Roumanian Royal Family

The Russian Royal Yacht *Standart*. (J & C McCutcheon Collection)

to arrange a marriage between the handsome Roumanian Crown Prince Carol and Grand Duchess Olga, eldest daughter of Tsar Nicholas II. Olga is reputed to have stated firmly, 'I'd rather die in Russia than marry him!' Tragically, she did, with many of her family during the 1917 Russian Revolution, being murdered at Ekaterinburg in 1918. A case of 'death before dishonour', considering the character and womanising career of Carol. The *Standart*, however, survived and was used by the Russian Navy as a minelayer, renamed *Marti* in 1917, refitted in 1930 and scrapped in 1963.

SPAIN

In 1898, Colonel Harry MacCalmont, the wealthy American yachtsman from whose estate the Portuguese government bought *Amelia* (III), ex-*Banshee*, in 1904, sold his 1,664-TM-ton, steel-hulled, twin-screw schooner *Giralda* to the Spanish government for use in the Spanish Navy as a despatch vessel. The three-masted, one-funnelled *Giralda* was built in 1894 by Fairfield Shipbuilding & Engineering Co., Govan, Glasgow, with a length of 289 feet, a beam of 35 feet and a draught of 18 feet. In addition, it was powered by two triple-expansion, six-cylinder steam engines fed by five boilers, producing 420 horsepower and giving a speed of 20 knots. On becoming king in 1902, King Alphonso XIII immediately used it for personal cruising and State purposes. It frequently attended the Cowes Week Regattas with King Alphonso, a member of the British Royal Yacht Squadron and related by marriage to Edward VII. He abdicated in 1931, and the Republican government used the vessel in their Navy as a survey ship, last recorded in such use in 1935. In the Science Museum, South Kensington, London, is a model of this ship.

King Alphonso XIII owned a 16-ton, International-Class, 10-metre, wooden-hulled, gaff-topsail cutter named *Tonino* that he raced in various regattas,

The Spanish Royal Yacht *Giralda*. (J & C McCutcheon Collection)

The Spanish Royal Yacht *Giralda* off Cowes. (J & C McCutcheon Collection)

The Spanish King's Yacht in harbour, Palma. (J & C McCutcheon Collection)

including Cowes. It was built by Astilleros del Nervion in 1911 at Bilbao, Spain, with a length of 43.75 feet, a beam of 9.34 feet and a draught of 6.3 feet. The sails were supplied by famous makers Ratsey & Lapthorn. He also owned the 15-metre *Hispania* and 6-metre *Barandil*. Another craft he owned was the 16-ton, 50-foot, twin-screw motor yacht *Fackung-Tu-Zinc*, built by S. E. Saunders Ltd, Cowes, in 1913. This vessel was powered by two Hispania Suiza eight-cylinder petrol engines driving the twin screws.

SWEDEN

The early Swedish royal yacht *Amphion* was notable because, if required, it could be powered by the crew rowing on oars. It was built in 1778 at Stockholm for King Gustav III, to the design of an Englishman, F. H. Chapman, as a 160-foot-long, two-masted, shallow-draught schooner. It was used most frequently for pleasure cruising in the Swedish and Finnish islands regions of the Baltic and also occasionally for ceremonial and festive purposes, but its special shallow draught meant it would not be comfortable aboard on the open sea. The carved decoration on the stern and the figurehead on the bows are known to be the work of the Swedish wood carver and sculptor Per Ljung. The figurehead is preserved in the Sjöhistoriska Museet (National Maritime Museum), Stockholm. After King Gustav III's death in 1792, *Amphion* was used as a depot ship and was finally broken up in 1885. In 1877, the iron-hulled, raked-two-masted, raked-two-funnelled, 630-TM-ton steam yacht *Ran* was built by Bergsunds Mekaniska Verstod, Stockholm. It had a length of 175 feet, a beam of 27 feet and a draught of 11 feet 5 inches, and was powered by compound steam engines driving a single-screw propeller, giving a speed of 12 knots. In 1883, it was renamed *Drott* and taken over as the Swedish royal yacht to be used by King Oscar I, followed by King Oscar II, a member of the British Royal Yacht Squadron, who does not appear to have used it to take part in Cowes Regatta. Instead he used the sailing yachts *Max*, of 22 tons, *Mathilda* of 25 tons and *Vanadis* of 40 tons, all in the Swedish Navy.

The figurehead carved by Per Ljung for the Swedish Royal Yacht *Amphion*, built in 1778. (Courtesy of the Sjöhistoriska Museet, National Maritime Museum, Stockholm)

YUGOSLAVIA

The 1,880-ton *Dubrovnik*, a torpedo boat destroyer in the Royal Yugoslavian Navy, also served as the country's royal yacht. It was built by Yarrow & Co. Poplar, London, in 1931 and had a length of 371 feet, a beam of 35 feet, a draught of 11 feet 7 inches, and was powered by Parsons geared turbines fed by three Yarrow boilers, producing 42,000 horsepower, giving a speed of 37 knots. It was chiefly used by King Alexander I and family for official visits to Turkey, Bulgaria and countries in that region. The aft accommodation was adapted for the use of the King and Queen on these visits. However, in October 1934, *Dubrovnik* conveyed the King from Yugoslavia for an official visit to France. While being driven from the harbour at Marseilles, King Alexander was assassinated by Croatian revolutionaries.

The Royal Yugoslavian Navy had two other ships on its strength used as royal yachts, mainly for pleasure cruises and short voyages. The 250-ton paddle-vessel *Dragor* had originally been an Austro-Hungarian patrol boat, but used as a royal yacht on the River Danube. The 230-ton, screw-yacht *Vila* was used to cruise among the Dalmatian islands. Upon King Alexander's murder, the royal yachts were designated for the use of Regent Prince Paul, but ceased to be used on the outbreak of war in 1939.

ROYAL YACHTS OUTSIDE EUROPE

EGYPT

The Egyptian iron-hulled, two-masted, one-funnelled screw-schooner *Mahroussa* had several career changes, refits and facelifts in its long life. It was built in 1865 at Samuda Brothers shipyard, Poplar, London, initially for the use of the Viceroy of Egypt. It had oscillating paddle steam engines built by John Penn & Sons, Blackheath, capable of 6,400 indicated horsepower, giving a speed of 18 knots. With a length of 400 feet, a beam of 42 feet and a draught of 17 feet 5 inches, it was the largest steam yacht in existence for a time. It was designed by Oliver Lang, a retired Royal Navy chief constructor. In 1905, at Glasgow, it was much altered and converted to screw propulsion with three triple-screw Parsons steam turbines capable of 6,500 horsepower, giving a speed of 17 knots. At this time it was also lengthened to 420 feet, its displacement being increased to 3,417 tons. At the end of the Second World War, it went into dry dock at La Spezia for an overhaul and again in 1950 for its funnel and upperworks to be updated.

Eventually, returning to its earlier career, it had come into the service of Ismail Pasha, Khedive of Egypt, then King Fuad, followed by his son King Farouk and President Nasser. Perhaps the career of the *Mahroussa* was most colourful during the reign of King Farouk, from 1936 to 1952, the King dying in 1965. For the honeymoon with his second wife, Narriman Sadek, on the royal yacht, Farouk had all the honeymoon party of some sixty people dressed in identical blue blazers, white ducks (trousers made of linen or cotton cloth worn in the tropics) and yachting caps. Increasingly unpopular, Farouk was arrested on the orders of a Revolutionary Command Council led by General Muhammed Neguib and Colonel Gamal al-Nasser, who was the power behind the military coup d'état. Half the Council wanted Farouk to be executed, but Nasser, who had a horror of murdering crimeless monarchs and others for political purposes, ordered Farouk to be freed. So the Council of army officers gave Farouk an ultimatum – either to abdicate or face imprisonment. He agreed to abdicate but only on condition that he could sail in state from Alexandria on his yacht *Mahroussa*, seen off by General Neguib, figurehead leader of the revolution against Farouk. In addition, as the *Mahroussa* left Alexandria there was to be a 21-gun royal salute, agreed to by the Council. Only after Farouk and his entourage had sailed away in the *Mahroussa* in July 1952 was it discovered that numerous trunks and packing cases stowed on the royal yacht were hoarded with gold taken from the vaults of the Bank of Egypt. The gold had been loaded into twelve ammunition boxes and the King's

The bow and figurehead of the Egyptian Royal Yacht *Mahroussa* in dry dock at La Spezia, at the end of the Second World War. (Courtesy of the La Spezia Museum, Italy. Author's Collection)

The Egyptian Royal Yacht *Mahroussa*, taken north of Suez sometime between 1945–50, possibly from naval tug HMS *Marauder* based at Malta. (Courtesy of R. W. Cowl, York. Author's collection)

servants had even gone to the Martazal Palace to fetch the valuable jewellery of Queen Narriman. However, some of the gold may have been legitimately owned by Farouk and Narriman, as all the wedding presents that had been in gold were secretly melted down into ingots shortly after the wedding. General Neguib, with a former Egyptian Prime Minister, Ali Maher, and the US Ambassador, Jefferson Cafferty, attended to say their farewells, after which the *Mahroussa* sailed to Naples, Capri and then Rome.

On learning of Farouk's actions some of the Revolutionary Command Council demanded *Mahroussa* should be bombed and sunk. However, Nasser overruled this scheme as well. In 2007, Princess Ferial Farouk revealed on Arab television that the same group in the Revolutionary Council, determined to put an end to the 200-year-old dynasty of Muhammed Ali and punish Farouk, had tried to torpedo *Mahroussa* on its way to Italy, and only failed to do so because of the skill of its Captain, who she called 'Le Prince de la Mer'. So *Mahroussa* safely sailed on, taking Farouk, Queen Narriman, Princesses Ferial, Fadia and Fawzia, and Prince Fouad into exile in Italy and Switzerland. The ship then returned to service in the Egyptian Navy as a training ship.

The next Egyptian royal yacht was the 669-TM-ton, steel-hulled, two-masted, one-funnelled screw-schooner *Safa-El-Bahr*, built in 1894 by A. & J. Inglis, Glasgow, for His Highness Khedive Abbas II of Egypt. It had a length of 221 feet, a beam of 27 feet and a draught of 12 feet, and was fitted with triple-expansion steam engines fed by two boilers, capable of 1,200 indicated horsepower, providing a speed of 14 knots. The Khedive used it mainly for pleasure cruises and, being pro-Turkish, which helped bring about his eventual downfall, frequent visits to the Sea of Marmara and Turkey. There is a model of *Safa-El-Bahr* in the Science Museum, South Kensington, London.

The 1,111-TM-ton, steel-hulled, two-masted, one-funnelled paddle-yacht *Kassed Kheir*, having a shallow draught of 3 feet 5 inches, was notably suitable for use on the Upper River Nile. It was designed and built by Messrs Thorneycroft, Southampton, in 1926. The instructions in the order stated that the vessel was to revive the glory days of Thomas Cook's Cruises on the Nile, with a vessel that contained furniture and fittings in the style of 'Victorian regal splendour' and that is what the customers got. It had a length of 237 feet 7 inches, a beam of 32 feet and a draught as stated, and was fitted with triple-expansion steam engines

Egyptian Royal Yacht. (J & C McCutcheon Collection)

driving the paddle wheels; the paddle boxes were ornately decorated with the Egyptian royal coat of arms. There was also extensive exterior decorations in a typical Arab style. It was constructed in sections, and then transported as deck cargo by ship to be assembled and launched on the Nile. Used by King Fuad and King Farouk, after the latter's exile, *Kassed Kheir* became a floating annexe for a hotel in Cairo. Another early Egyptian royal yacht was the aptly named *Cleopatra*, built in 1853 for HRH Il Rama Pasha, but little is known about it.

TURKEY

Although a country positioned on the crossroads of Europe and Asia, the rulers of Turkey still felt the nation should be equal to both, and in this respect the Sultan should have a royal yacht. So in 1898, the 78-ton, single-screw *Teshrifiyeh* was built in a Turkish shipyard for Sultan Abdul Hamid. In 1903, this was supplemented by a screw-propelled barge, *Seughudlu*, built by Armstrong Whitworth & Co. Newcastle-on-Tyne. In 1904, the 964-ton, three-masted, two-funnelled, steel-hulled, twin-screw schooner *Erthogroul* was also built there by Armstrong Whitworth & Co., with a length of 264 feet, a beam of 27 feet and a draught of 14 feet. It was powered by two triple-expansion, six-cylinder steam

The Royal Yacht *Erthogroul*, which was used by the Sultan of Turkey, *c.* 1900. (Courtesy of Tomaso Gropallo, Genoa, Italy. Author's collection)

Turkish Royal Yacht *Savarona*, 9 May 1953.

engines giving 144 horsepower, the engines built by Hawthorn, Leslie & Co., Newcastle. Sultan Mohammed V continued to use *Erthogroul* from 1909 until 1918 when he was deposed.

The next Turkish example was the 4,317-ton, two-funnelled *Savarona*, built Hamburg in about 1928 for the Cadwaladar family of Philadelphia, this being the traditional name for the yachts owned by this family. In 1938, it was sold by them and eventually given to President Inonu of Turkey for his use as the Turkish Presidential Yacht; *Savarona* was the largest private steam yacht built up to that time. Another source states that it was bought 'in the 1930s' and used by President Ataturk until his death in 1938, when it became 'such a vessel for President Inonu'. In May 1946, President Inonu offered use of *Savarona* to take King Faisal II, the Queen Mother Aliya and others of the Iraqi Royal Family, including the Queen Grandmother Nafisa and three princesses who were now King Faisal's aunts, from Alexandretta, now Iskenderun, to Marseilles en route to England for a summer holiday. It sailed from Alexandretta on 29 May 1946 arriving at Marseilles on 6 June, where the royal party disembarked. The *Savarona* was described as 'a floating luxury hotel', the architecture and furnishings being representative of a grand building more so than a seagoing ship, even though a Presidential Yacht, the service and food 'flawless' and the Turkish wines were 'excellent.'

ZANZIBAR

Even the Sultan of Zanzibar had his own 'royal yacht', *Nyanza*, although it was not quite a vessel usually covered by that terminology. The 2,082-ton *Nyanza* was a two-funnelled, paddle-wheel steamship when built for the P&O Line in 1864. In 1874, the P&O Line sold it to the Union Line Steamship Company for the latter to expand their Southampton to Cape Town mail service. The Union Line had it converted to screw propulsion, removed a funnel and lengthened it by 17 feet.

It served well on this primary mail service route, but was eventually replaced by faster ships. So in 1880, it was assigned with other 'declassd' older liners to the Cape Town to East Africa service, to support other smaller, older and slower ships pioneering this new service. In 1880, it made a first visit to the island of Zanzibar. The Sultan of Zanzibar, Bargh-ash-Selim, saw the arrival of *Nyanza* and went on board. He admired it, so he bought it and used it as his private royal yacht. In 1882, *Nyanza*, with the Sultan's Special Envoy on board, made a special voyage from Zanzibar to London. The Envoy had with him two ivory tusks that he had to deliver 'in person' to the then-chairman of the Union Line Steamship Company at his house in Portman Square, London. When not being used by the Sultan as his royal yacht, it sailed between Zanzibar and Bombay, India, with passengers, mail and cargo. Eventually, its sailing days came to an end, but *Nyanza* remained a familiar sight anchored off the Zanzibar waterfront. Like the sentiments of Queen Victoria and King Edward VII in respect of *Victoria and Albert* (III), Sultan Bargh-ash-Selim was still so enamoured of his royal yacht he could not bring himself to dispose of it. Locally it was designated 'His Highness's Saluting and Signalling Ship, *Nyanza*', until inevitably in 1904 the *Nyanza* was reluctantly sent to the ship-breakers.

PRESIDENTIAL, STATE AND MISCELLANEOUS YACHTS

ARGENTINE REPUBLIC

The *Presidente Sarmiento* was built in 1897 by Cammell Laird & Co., Birkenhead, and launched on 31 August, being nicknamed 'Sarah Me Auntie' by the shipyard men who could not pronounce its name. This two-funnelled, three-masted frigate was an Argentine Navy cadet training ship for many years until converted to a Presidential Yacht.

THE UNITED STATES OF AMERICA

Since the United States Administration of President Rutherford Hayes (1877–81) a yacht has been maintained and operated by the US Navy for the use of the President. The 1,780-gross-ton luxury steam yacht *Mayflower* was built by J. & G. Thompson, Glasgow, in 1896, for a private owner, Ogden Coelet. It had a length of 273 feet, a beam of 36 feet, and a draught of 17 feet 2 inches, and was armed with six six-pounder guns. Its vertical triple-expansion engines were powered by two Mosher boilers driving the twin-screw ship at 16.8 knots. In 1898, *Mayflower* was purchased by the US Government as a gunboat for service off Cuba in the Spanish–American War. During this conflict, the crew boarded a British merchant ship, also named *Mayflower*, which was being used as a blockade runner, and sent it to the United States with a prize crew aboard. After service at Puerto Rico and Santo Domingo in 1906, *Mayflower* was assigned to be the President's yacht. It was used successively by Presidents Theodore Roosevelt, Taft, Harding and Coolidge, until laid up by President Hoover in 1929. Many members of the world's royalty and governments visited *Mayflower* and signed its guest book. At League Island Navy Yard, Philadelphia, on 24 January 1931, it caught fire and was badly damaged. It was privately purchased in 1931 and restored. In 1942, the US War Shipping Administration bought it from Broadfoot Iron Works, Wilmington, North Carolina, to be converted to a wartime Coast Guard ship used for radar training. It was decommissioned in 1946 and was sold into private ownership in January 1947.

The USS *Despatch, Dolphin and Sylph* were also US Navy ships used by presidents. The *Despatch* was originally the steamship *America*, bought by the US Government in November 1873. It had a length of 174 feet, a beam of 25 feet 6 inches, a draught of 12 feet 4 inches, and a tonnage of 560, and was armed with three twenty-pounder guns. During the war with Spain, it served on the North Atlantic Station until 1877, when assigned to special duty with the US Embassy in Constantinople, Turkey, as a means of conveying the American Minister to Turkey during a time of internal unrest and a state of war with Russia. From 1880 to 1891, it served on special assignments, including conveying the President and Cabinet members to fleet reviews, celebrations and ceremonies. In August 1891, *Despatch* conveyed the Secretary of the Navy to review the North Atlantic Fleet and the Squadron of Evolution. On 10 October 1891, during a gale, *Despatch* was wrecked on Assateague Island off the Virginia coast, but all officers and crew got ashore safely. The USS *Dolphin*, a cruiser built by John Roach & Sons, Chester, Pennsylvania, and launched in December 1885, had a length of 256 feet 6 inches, a beam of 32 feet, a draught of 14 feet 3 inches and a displacement of 1,486 tons. Its vertical compound engine was powered by two double-ended and two single-ended cylindrical engines driving the single-screw ship at 16 knots. Armed with two 4-inch/40-calibre guns and five three-pounder guns, *Dolphin* served on the North Atlantic Station until 1886, when it was reassigned to the Pacific Station visiting Japan, Korea, China, Ceylon, India, Arabia, Egypt, Italy, Spain, England, arriving in New York in 1889. From 1899 to 1914, *Dolphin* was used as a special duties ship often carrying the President and government officials, and important mail and dispatches. During the First World War, it patrolled the Caribbean, protecting American and British interests. After the war, *Dolphin* was used on a wide range of duties, including representing the United States at a celebration of the 400th anniversary of the discovery of the Straits of Magellan. It was decommissioned in December 1921 and sold in February 1922.

The USS *Sylph* was built by John Roach, Chester, Pennsylvania, in 1898, and that year bought by the United States Navy. It had a waterline length of 123 feet 8 inches, a beam of 20 feet, a mean draught of 7 feet 6 inches, and was armed with six six-pounders and two three-pounders. Its vertical triple-expansion engine drove the single-screw converted yacht at 15 knots. President McKinley was the first to use *Sylph* as a Presidential Yacht. President Theodore Roosevelt cruised on *Sylph* to his summer residence at Oyster Bay, New York, and President Taft used it for summer cruises off the New England coast. *Sylph* also carried distinguished passengers on short cruises and sight-seeing excursions of the Potomac River and Chesapeake Bay. At that time the King of the Belgians and the Crown Prince of Sweden were among many royal passengers and distinguished statesmen who enjoyed its service. President Woodrow Wilson was the last President to use *Sylph*. After this it had a number of varied duties, but was decommissioned in April 1929 and sold to a private owner in November that year.

President Franklin D. Roosevelt used the 100-ton, wooden motor yacht *Sequoia*, built in 1925 for a private owner by the Mathis Yacht Shipbuilding Company, Camden, New Jersey. It had an overall length of 104 feet, a beam of 19 feet, a draught of 4 feet 5 inches, a speed of 12 knots, and no armament. The Navy Department acquired it in March 1933. From then until 1935, President Roosevelt used *Sequoia* for official and pleasure cruises, and it was used by successive Presidents as the main Presidential Yacht until President Carter decided it was 'a wasteful extravagance', selling it to a Trust to preserve. However, it was still used by presidents until 1991, when it was taken over by Norfolk Virginia Shipyard for financial reasons. In 2000, a group of investors acquired it. President Roosevelt used the 415-ton USS *Potomac* in 1936. Built at the Manitowoc Shipbuilding Corporation in 1934, it had an overall length of 165 feet, an extreme beam of 23 feet 9 inches, a draught of 8 feet 7 inches, and two diesel engines giving it a speed of 13 knots. It was decommissioned in November 1941 after which it had various owners, one being Elvis Presley, another a Warren G. Toone who used it as a passenger ferry service in the Caribbean.

Another Presidential Yacht was the 1,920-ton USS *Williamsburg* built in 1931 by the Bath Iron Works, Bath, Maine, as *Aras* for a private owner. It had an overall length of 243 feet 9 inches, an extreme beam of 36 feet, a draught of 16 feet, and diesel engines giving it a speed of 16 knots. In 1941, it was bought by the United States Navy, renamed *Williamsburg* and converted to a gunboat with 3-inch, 50-calibre guns, being used in wartime convoy service. In 1945, it was assigned as a Presidential Yacht for President Harry S. Truman. One notable occasion was the arrival of Prime Minister Winston Churchill for dinner with the President in January 1952. Decommissioned in 1953, *Williamsburg* was converted in 1962 into a fully equipped biological US research ship and used from 1963 to 1965 on a research cruise as part of the International Indian Ocean Expedition, being named *Anton Brunn* in honour of a notable Danish marine biologist. For this conversion, presidential staterooms and other rooms and fittings were removed and laboratories and aquaria tanks replaced them.

It is traditional for each new US President to rename the Presidential yachts. A 64-foot cabin cruiser built in 1940 by Fisher Boat Works at Detroit for a private owner was acquired by the Coast Guard in 1942, transferred to the US Navy in 1945 and used by some presidents. First it was named *Dollar*, then *Margie*. President Truman renamed it *Margaret T*; President Eisenhower renamed it *Susan Elaine*; President Kennedy renamed it *Patrick J*; and President Nixon renamed it *Julie*. Put on sale in 1969, but unsold, it was decommissioned in 1970. The Presidential yacht *Lenore* was built by the Defoe Boat Works, Bay City, Michigan, in 1931, for private ownership. It had a length of 92 feet 3 inches, and a beam of 16 feet 6 inches. In 1942, it was bought by the US War Shipping Administration for the US Coast Guard. It was later transferred to the US Navy as *Lenore* (II) in 1945 and frequently conveyed the Secret Service men accompanying the President on his official voyages and pleasure cruises. In 1953, it was refurnished and assigned as a Presidential yacht. President Eisenhower renamed it *Barbara Anne* in honour of his granddaughter, but mainly used it to take him from his Newport summer headquarters to and from his golfing excursions. In March 1961, President Kennedy renamed it *Honey Fitz*, after his maternal grandfather John Francis Fitzgerald.

Extravagance: the *Sequoia* was the official presidential yacht from 1933 until Jimmy Carter ordered its sale in 1977. (*The Sunday Telegraph*)

BIBLIOGRAPHY

Cooke, John (text), *The Royal Yacht Britannia Official Guidebook* (Someone Publishing Ltd. Royal Yacht Britannia Trust, Edinburgh).

Crabtree, Reginald, *Royal Yachts of Europe* (David & Charles, 1975).

Dalglish, Commander J. S., *The Life Story of a Fish* (The Adelphi Press, 1992). Autobiography, known as Fish from his nickname at Dartmouth Naval College.

Dalton, Tony, *British Royal Yachts* (Halsgrove, 2002). The classic book of in-depth coverage of the planning, construction and career of the Royal Yacht *Britannia*, among former examples, and the minutiae of shipboard life of that time and various plans for after decommissioning, including a refit or alternative new Royal Yacht.

Gavin, Commander C. E., *Royal Yachts* (Rich & Cowan, 1932). The classic book on the history of British Royal Yachts up to the year of publication.

Underhill, Harold A., *Sailing Ship Rigs and Rigging* (Brown, Son & Ferguson).

Magazine articles:

Fitzroy, Angela, 'The Story of the *Victoria & Albert* Floating Home of the Royal Family', *Portsmouth Evening Herald*, 20 July 1936.

Griffith, Mrs M., 'The Queen's Yacht', *The Strand Magazine*, 1894. (By special permission of Her Majesty, Queen Victoria.)

Lapthorn, W. H., 'Statenjachts', *Motor Boat & Yachting*, May 1970.

'R. M.', 'The Royal Yacht *Victoria and Albert*', *Model Boats*, December 1970.

'When Royalty Go Afloat' (no writer named) *Silver Jubilee Naval Supplement*, 1935. (No publisher stated.